SHIPWRECKS & RESCUES

Forgotten Great Lakes History

WES OLESZEWSKI

Avery Color Studios, Inc.
Gwinn, Michigan

©2008 Avery Color Studios, Inc.

ISBN-13: 978-1-892384-46-1
ISBN-10: 1-892384-46-9

Library of Congress Control Number: 2007943891

First Edition 2008
10   9   8   7   6   5   4   3   2   1

Published by
Avery Color Studios, Inc.
Gwinn, Michigan 49841

Cover photos: top photo by Terry Charbeneau, bottom photo by Shelley Vickers

To Walt Oleszewski
My dad,

Of all the members of my family, my dad is the only person who has read every single one of my books cover-to-cover. This will be the first book that he will be unable to read. Dad passed away in December 2004.

My dad loved to tag along on book signings with me and research trips around the lakes. He was supportive in every venture that I undertook and never one to scoff and quip "you can't do that." Rather dad was one to say "Try it and see." He was a skilled railroad engineer, yet his favored job was driving the Zamboni ice resurfacer for the Saginaw Gears hockey team. One of my fondest memories of my youth was the privilege of skating on dad's perfect ice. Until the time when we meet again, I will miss skating on my dad's perfect ice and I will miss my best and most loyal reader.

My dad, circa 1975, in his prime working his zamboni.

TABLE OF CONTENTS

FOREWORD

Having taken a three year break in order to begin the process of being a parent, I return to the area of Great Lakes Maritime history with great delight. Once the process of making this book was underway, my publisher informed me that my third book, *Ice Water Museum*, was going out of print. The desire to preserve some of my favorite stories from that text led to them being included here. They have been, of course, updated and greater detail has been added. This is a direct result of having published ten books in between then and now. I have better sources and resources now, plus a lot of discoveries have been made in the world of Great Lakes shipwrecks. Many of the stories in that third book are now out of date and really need to be rewritten.

Additionally, I have been researching a few hundred stories of the ships and people of the lakes. From that pile I have selected the most fun (for me at least) tales to tell and placed them into this text. As always, every story is true and as highly researched as I can make them. If a fact could not be checked, I'll tell you that in the text.

Keep in mind that these are historical narratives and that the events that you are reading really took place. If you visit the places where these stories took place you will find yourself walking or wading in the same places where the persons in these stories trekked. I often go to the locations where the tales are based and stand where the people stood who built the boats, sailed the boats, rescued the crews and waved goodbye to the crews. My rule is that in order to know the events, we must understand the people.

Above all, however, it is my job to tell the stories of the obscured events and the forgotten adventures of the lakes and to take you, the reader, there. Let these pages be the amazing machine that teleports you through time and space and places you amid the adventures documented here.

ARE THEY GHOSTS?

From the predawn darkness the lights of a vessel appeared. She was a small boat as her lamps revealed and the crew of the shipwrecked steamer *Ohio*, adrift in a tiny lifeboat without so much as a paddle shouted and waved in desperation and joy, then watched in horror as the little vessel simply sailed right by, passing like a specter within 200-feet of their yawl. Once again they were left alone and adrift in the middle of Lake Erie with only the hope of rescue to keep them going. Shortly after the little ghost ship vanished into the distance, another small vessel came bearing down toward the castaways. This time they shouted louder and waved even more vigorously and once again they watched as the small vessel passed within 165-feet of their yawl but never seemed to see them. To the crew of the *Ohio* it must have seemed as if either these were ghost ships or that the men themselves were the ghosts. Perhaps it was they who did not survive the *Ohio's* demise and they were now doomed to spend eternity drifting upon Lake Erie forever beckoning toward passing boats who would never see their signals.

By the end of 1859, the port city of Buffalo, New York was already a bustling metropolis of marine commerce. To the west, across Lake Erie, anything west and north of Detroit was still largely a frontier. Even the city of Chicago was still considered to be way out west. Thus Buffalo was the transit point for moving the materials for the frontier west and for receiving the ever growing grain and newly cut lumber east. With the locks at Sault Saint Marie having been opened just four years earlier, the path to the great wilderness of Lake Superior and the wonders of its shores was now wide open and thus led to even greater traffic through the Buffalo artery. This was a time when railroads had hardly established routes beyond Cleveland, leaving the path of best transportation west by lakeboat. Buffalo's waterfront was a place where stacks of cordwood to fuel steamboats was jumbled with warehouses and depots meant to fill whatever hull could be hired to haul the equipment, dry goods, and people west. Hooting whistles filled the air as the shouts and whistles of dock workers mixed with the noise and horses snorted as wagons waited and were loaded or unloaded. From April until late November the activity was non-stop.

In this era, Buffalo was a place where fortunes could be made, careers could be started, and great men could be found beginning to pay their dues. Standing on the docks in this period was a cocky, bearded 18-year old

Scotsman by the name of James Davidson who was a prime example of how one could rise in the ranks of the Buffalo waterfront. An orphan, Davidson had started to support himself on the Buffalo waterfront at the age of 11 by using his rowboat to taxi people to and from vessels in the harbor. By November of 1859 he was looking toward getting his first command of a real lakeboat the following spring. He would go on to a magnificent career on the lakes, owning his own fleet of wooden lakers. Likewise many other young men strode along the docks and bulkheads of Buffalo and sailed out of the port with success in their future. Some, however, boarded vessels and sailed out of port and found a cruel, cold disaster in their future. Many of those were simply never seen again. Still, there were others to whom the harbor and the lake was simply a place to do an honest day's work, in spite of the danger and with little regard for the beckoning of distant fortune. Some of those were members of the Nickerson family.

Residents of the harbor of Buffalo were quite used to seeing all sorts of people disembarking at the train stations. From dapper ladies and gentlemen to ragamuffin transients, the harbor town and its booming economy attracted every sort of person. So it was that few took particular notice of the two ragamuffins who stepped from the westbound train on the morning of Tuesday, November 8th, 1859. Perhaps they would have taken notice had anyone known that the man and the boy dressed in ill-fitting, second hand shoes, using well worn blankets for jackets and looking as if they had spent the night riding on top of the rail car rather than inside it, were none other than Captain David Phillipe Nickerson and his 16-year old son Vincent. Together the two Nickerson men trudged from the rail station and headed toward their Buffalo home. They had departed Buffalo just four days previous in a far better state of well being. Now they returned having lost their jobs, most of their possessions and a sizable portion of their pride. Yet they knew that this job of working on the lakes had the potential to take much more than that from them. This time, they had once again returned with their lives.

Just before 10:00 am on the previous Friday, Captain Nickerson was in command of the wooden steamer *Ohio* as she headed out of Buffalo harbor bound for Cleveland. The *Ohio* was everything short of being a "new" boat. In fact, she currently was winding up her 29th season of toil on the lakes and it was common knowledge that her wooden timbers were a bit "ripe." In the able hands of the 51-year old Captain Nickerson, however, the vessel's tender hull was not a problem. He treated her well, stuck close to the shore in the spring and autumn sailing seasons and was known to find cover whenever the gale winds came blowing. The *Ohio*, although considered large when she was launched in Sandusky, Ohio, had slipped to the ranks of medium size three decades later. Measuring 107-feet long and 20-feet in beam the boat drew a modest 8-feet of water. Her screw propeller drove her along at a top

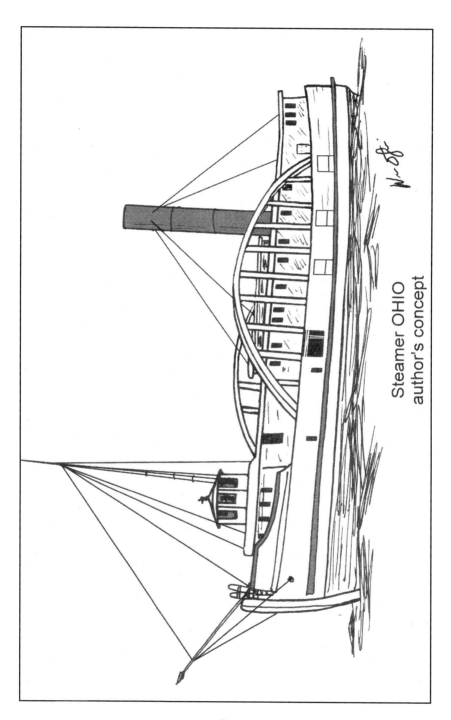

Steamer OHIO
author's concept

speed of just over seven miles per hour. She carried two masts and a set of sails to aid her in making a bit better speed as she cleared Buffalo that Friday morning. Captain Nickerson found the winds favoring putting out the forward jib sail. With her belly filled with 350 tons of merchandise of every sort, the deeply laden old steamer would need every bit of help that the good captain could offer.

No sooner had the triangular jib been fully set than Captain Nickerson took the opportunity to go down to Vincent's cabin to check on his son. Vincent had been stricken with a case of "fever" which would be the mid 1800's description of many types of illness or infection that would result in someone running a high temperature. Still even in his weakened state, young Vincent refused to not ship out with his father. On returning to the pilothouse, Captain Nickerson could not help but stick his chest out a bit; his boy was growing into a real mariner. Nothing was going to keep him on the beach, not even a terrible fever. Of course that pride was tempered with the memory of eldest son Andrew. In 1852 while the good captain was in command of the schooner *Mary*, 19-year-old Andrew had shipped aboard to serve as cook, while 9-year-old Vincent was sailing for his very first season as the cabin boy. As the *Mary* was making her way along the Detroit River, one of her booms came loose and swung wildly, striking Andrew and knocking him overboard into the swift blue currents of the river. The Detroit River took him and never gave him back. Much like the fever, the loss of his older brother did not deter Vincent from a life of sailing the lakes.

Of course the lakes had already taken a turn at Vincent. Following his birth on October 7, 1843 his father was well established as a lakes captain serving as commander of side-wheel steamers *Eclipse* and *Bunker Hill*. Young Vincent was taken aboard one of his father's commands as an infant and placed in the captain's stateroom bunk. Cradled in a soft oversized pillow, the tiny baby was quite comfortable, that is until the jib boom of the brig *Commerce* came crashing through the wall! The brig had collided with Captain Nickerson's steamer right at the captain's cabin. Like a pancake spatula, the brig's jib slid beneath the slumbering newborn baby and scooped him up, pillow and all. Then as the lake and the dynamics of collision worked upon the two massive wooden lakeboats forcing them apart, the *Commerce's* boom began to withdraw. With it, the boom took the infant, pillow and all. Through the thicket of shattered hull timbers the boom pulled the baby. Any one of the thousands of slivers could have snagged the baby or the pillow, dumping the helpless infant into the dark cold waters of the lake and to a certain death. Amazingly, the baby and pillow were cleanly extracted through the hole. Wheelsman Joseph Dunn spotted the baby squirming in that precarious roost and using his instinctive mariner's climbing skills, he made his way through the wreckage toward the baby. Any misstep or awkward tug on the lines or stays could easily dump baby

Vincent into the lake. Vincent's luck held, however, and he was plucked from danger and returned to the arms of his terrified mother. Sixteen years later, Vincent was again sleeping peacefully on another of his father's commands unaware that the lakes were stalking him once more.

Through the day the *Ohio* huffed along at her snail's pace. As the day wore on, November began to show her teeth. Captain Nickerson being well aware of his vessel's age and tender hull was not in the mood to take any chances. Running west by south and three quarters south along the north shore of Lake Erie, he had been in the lee of the land. Tapping his brand new barometer, Captain Nickerson sensed the winds were showing a tendency to shift in an ill direction. As the boat passed Point Abino, Captain Nickerson ordered the wheelsman to begin steering west northwest and head for the shelter of Gravely Bay. Just over nine miles later, the *Ohio* dropped her hooks into the sandy bottom and waited for better winds.

By the time the *Ohio's* cook was placing dinner on the table the winds were fading and Captain Nickerson ordered her anchors raised. With that, the steamer hissed out of Gravely Bay and continued on her way southwest toward Cleveland. By 11 o'clock that evening the *Ohio* was abeam Long Point and making good weather of it. Three and a quarter hours later, Captain Nickerson was hollow eyed as he left the pilot house in charge of the wheelsman. He made his way down to the *Ohio's* engine room. There he found everything to be in good shape. The boiler's pressure read 65 pounds of head steam, the second engineer was busy oiling the machinery and the fireman was tending to the boiler's water, which he reported to the captain that everything was "all right."

Stepping up on deck Captain Nickerson took a long look across the lake. The autumn night was crystal clear and he judged her position as being 30 miles above Long Point and 10 miles from shore. The weather had turned quite fair which served to relax the exhausted master and that, along with his crew's confident reports allowed Captain Nickerson to retire to his quarters for a well earned nap. No Great Lakes vessel master of this era would actually crawl beneath the covers and curl up to sleep in his pajamas while his boat was underway. There were just too many hazards lurking on the open lake. So it was that Captain Nickerson shut his cabin door and taking off his hat, coat and boots he lounged on top of his neatly made bed. With the coming day's business running through his mind he relaxed, awake for several minutes. Then came a deafening explosion and a shock wave jolted him from his bed. Instinctively he bounded out through his cabin door.

What Captain Nickerson saw as he stepped onto what remained of the *Ohio's* deck was a nightmare come true. The air was thick with a haze of filthy steam and a million glowing orange sparks swirled everywhere like angry fireflies. There was nothing left of the *Ohio* aft of his toes and above the level of the hurricane deck. Before his heart could hammer its next beat huge pieces of the ship began to rain from the sky, splashing into the lake all around him. Then the cries and shouts of his crew struggling in the water were heard as the good captain felt the timbers beneath his feet begin to sink. In a state of shock he stood there until one of the *Ohio's* yawl boats came tumbling down from the night's sky and landed right side up in the water just past the rail where his hand was resting. He instinctively thought to stay with his ship and see if there was any way to save her. Turning toward the bow, as if to evaluate her condition, he saw that everything forward of his position was intact, but aft of where he stood there was only wreckage. He attempted to call the names of crewmen, but heard only cries for help in return. He tried to move wreckage as if his own hands could save his boat, but was met with tons of shattered wood. Soon it was clear that his only duty remaining was to get into that yawl and start pulling what remained of his crew out of the water. He simply stepped into the lifeboat as the *Ohio* sunk.

As the captain pulled survivors from the lake, those rescued reached for their fellow crewmen. The captain's son Vincent had been trapped beneath his cabin roof as everything around him collapsed in the explosion, but he was rescued by the chief engineer who reached through the wreckage to pull him free. Soon the crewmembers of the propeller *Ohio* were aboard the tiny yawl boat. Loaded beyond capacity, the little boat had just a few inches of freeboard and

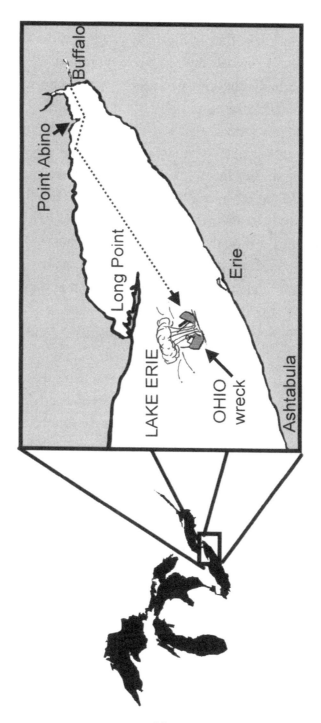

everyone knew that if the lake kicked up again, they could easily end up back in the frigid water.

In the blackness of open Lake Erie, the crew of the *Ohio* took a head count. Two men were missing and a century and a half later, we still are not sure of their names. One of the missing men was the *Ohio's* wheelsman whose name history records as being "Michael Donegan" or "Michael Danigan" or "Charles Banagen." The other missing mariner, the boat's second mate, has his name recorded as "Thomas Corvett" and "Thomas Corbett" and simply "Curvette." Although we cannot say for sure today what the actual names of these men were, you can bet that their correct names were shouted into the dark a hundred times that night. To these shouts there would, however, never come a response. Their names would be swallowed by the blackness of the lake as effectively as their identities were swallowed by history. There was word that the second mate had been seen running aft right after the explosion, but no one knew what had become of the wheelsman. Much like the *Ohio* herself, both men were simply gone. Now those who remained alive were left bobbing in a tiny wooden boat waiting for Lake Erie to deliver their fate.

What happened to the *Ohio* was an all to common fate for steam vessels of her era; it was a boiler explosion. Steam power came to the lakes in the first decade of the 1800s. Following the War of 1812 there was a small expansion in the number of Great Lakes steamers. In 1820 there were only four steamboats operating on the lakes. In the decade that followed eight more steamers were built on the freshwater seas, including small craft. In the decade of the 1830s, however, more than 80 new steamboats were constructed and placed in service, including the *Ohio*. Thus the construction rate increased by more than ten fold in just one decade. The problem was that making steamboats, especially their boilers, was not an exact engineering science. In fact, marine boiler making was about as far away from engineering science as it could get. There were no real design specifications and limitations such as the thickness of the steel walls used, the girth of the fittings applied and even the quality of the materials were left up to guess work and limited prior experience. A person actually needed to do little more than say he was a boilermaker to set up shop and begin manufacturing boilers for vessels. Steam power for railroads developed on nearly a parallel timeline as that used in lakeboats so the entire technology was very new. Add this to the pressures of demand for lake steamers and what you have is a very dangerous combination of a new technology pressed into service in a transportation mode that carried hundreds of people. To make matters worse, the actual physics of how a steam power plant functioned as well as how it may degrade with use were not understood. The use of pressure figures for gages simply read numbers that meant that nothing had yet blown up at that particular pressure, so it must be good. There was no understanding of the fact that heating and cooling, pressurizing and depressurizing caused the strength of the boiler's metal plating and parts to actually weaken and that most of the stress problems caused by these repeated cycles were invisible and at a molecular level in the metal. It was unknown that such weaknesses would not become apparent until the instant that the metal failed and the boiler exploded. No one actually had any data on what the useful life of a given boiler should be, because every boiler was made and had individual characteristics. With no real science, testing or standards, as long as a boiler held water and maintained pressure it was good for another season, or until it exploded, whichever came first. Such was the case with the *Ohio* and her boiler; no one suspected that it would explode.

Drifting across the expanse of open Lake Erie, the survivors of the *Ohio* had little thought of the history of boiler development. Their only thought was that of rescue and the hope that some passing vessel would stumble upon them. They had no oars and were using a few pieces of the *Ohio's* shattered hull timbers to attempt to propel their tiny boat. The point in rowing was quite moot, however, since no one really knew exactly which direction would be the best. Still, the act of attempting to row kept spirits up and no one reminded themselves of the hopelessness of this activity.

In the depth of that night, in the darkness before dawn was when the *Ohio's* survivors encountered the two small vessels that simply passed within 200-feet of them yet never seemed to notice. It was a chilling feeling for the castaways to be passed by in spite of their loud shouts and frantic waving. The feeling that they were caught up in some sort of ghost ship encounter was easily spun. Of course there is a good explanation as to why they were passed by and it has more to do with the normal than the paranormal. In the 1859 era, small vessels such as the two that passed the castaways, were often crewed by as few as two or three including the captain. Often when the boat was in the open lake, it was not unheard of for the wheel to be lashed on course and the boat to be left on her own as the wheelsman caught a nap. Concepts such as having a watchman standing duty were nonexistent on such boats and the odds are that if either of these two boats had anyone at all at their wheel, he was either sleeping, or drunk, or both.

By daylight the wind began to kick up toward gale strength and the temperatures began to drop. Lake Erie's surface had turned into a nasty chop and the overcrowded yawl began to take water over the side. By noon the winds were blowing full gale and for the next two hours the seas ran higher than Captain Nickerson had ever seen on the lakes. Using whatever they could, from hats to cupped hands, the *Ohio's* crew began to bail. Most of the survivors were wearing little more than what they had on when they went to bed, so many were without shoes and nearly all were without jackets. To make the situation worse they had nearly all received a bath in Lake Erie's ice water before being pulled into the yawl, so every stitch of clothing was wet and there was no way to dry off.

Most of the normally bustling lake traffic had retired for the winter by early November of 1859 so as the day went on, there were only two vessels spotted. The first was a propeller that moved along only half way above the horizon and then slipped off toward a distant port. Next came a sailing vessel that popped over the horizon, but veered off toward land. As night began to cover the lake the mood among the *Ohio's* crew became grim. The night would almost certainly bring their doom as the temperatures would continue to drop and their little lifeboat could easily be swamped by any given wave. It was now that the leadership that only a man like Captain Nickerson can muster, began to show. He bellowed encouragements and enlisted the aid of his most spirited crew to keep the others busy. He ordered them to bail and not to let the lake get the better of them. He reminded them that they had taken the worst this trip could offer and they could use the old *Ohio's* timbers to paddle to Detroit if they had to. The autumn darkness came early and the brave captain lead his crew into it believing that they would survive by their will alone.

No sooner had the gray autumn sky swallowed the sun than the lights of a steamer were seen in the distance. Captain Nickerson commanded that they would not be passed up this time, his men believed him and indeed this time the steamer's whistle hooted in response to their waving arms and shouted cries. The

650-ton two year old steamer *Equator* hovered up to the windward of the yawl, providing lee with her massive hull as her crew plucked the *Ohio's* survivors from the clutches of Lake Erie.

Aboard the *Equator*, Captain Nickerson and his men were treated to every comfort that the boat could offer from heated spirits to warm blankets and second-hand, but dry clothing. As the *Equator* headed west to Sandusky, the men of the *Ohio* listened to the wind screaming through her rigging and knew how lucky they were to have dry feet and not to be ghosts of Lake Erie. Once in port, most of the *Ohio's* crew caught the train for Buffalo. They were indeed a rag-tag bunch, unshaven with ill fitting clothing and some still wearing blankets from the *Equator*, but they were not ghosts and that was for certain. When they arrived home they appeared at their door at about the expected time, but with the news that the entire family was out of work, at least for the next few months.

Captain Nickerson went on to manage vessels in the Buffalo and Cleveland area and remained in the maritime industry until his death in 1892. His young son Vincent went on to work aboard several Great Lakes schooners and steamers. He must have gotten his father's blood for adventure as he joined the US Navy during the Civil War. Following that he sailed the oceans and was thereby involved in another shipwreck while aboard the *Valeria* when that vessel was wrecked off the coast of Brazil. The ship was repaired and Vincent, along with his shipmates, returned aboard her to the United States. He also sailed around the horn and when in San Francisco jumped ship and took a crack at gold mining and doing marine art. He later returned to the lakes and settled in Cleveland where he continued his art career and also helped his father in the management of vessels.

Too often the lakes have taken adventuresome and brave mariners and consumed them leaving not a human trace. They become nothing more than ghosts upon the lake, beckoning in vain across the waves of history waiting for us to find them. Yet for Captain Nickerson and his son Vincent, such a fate was not to be. The lakes had their turn at them but these two mariners were not about to become ghosts, they were not ghosts and that was for certain.

DOG BARKIN'

Within the pilothouse, Captain John Massy was clad only in short sleeves, pants and his favorite worn-out slippers as he peered from the open window into Lake Superior's night. For just an instant, he felt a strange presence hovering over his shoulder, as if sensing the gravity of someone who had walked silently close and was now standing behind him. He turned quickly toward the empty presence, half expecting to find one of the crew standing close by in the darkened wheelhouse, but there was no one. An instant later, his attention was drawn to the starboard window where the foggy blackness had suddenly brightened. Before his heart could beat again, Captain Massy was at the whistle pull. Putting his weight to it, he yanked a number of quick tugs commanding his boat's whistle to sound the danger signal. Like a giant freshwater sea monster, another lakeboat rose from the fog, surrounded by the amber glow of her lights and charged directly at the electrified master's boat. There was time for nothing more than that short danger signal from the boat's whistle, before the two steel lake giants bit into one another with a deafening roar. It became the same scene of horror played too often on the cobalt blue waters off Whitefish Point, the closing act of a story that could be aptly titled "Death of a Lakeboat." Tonight's performance was culminating at midnight, on the ninth day of July 1911.

This story has its true beginning four years before Captain Massy had that strange feeling and saw the lights in the fog. At the Great Lakes Engineering Works in St. Clair, Michigan, the 440-foot steel hull, designated number 25, hit fresh water. The year was 1907 and hull 25 was christened *John Mitchell*. When she entered service the *Mitchell* was nothing special to look at. Actually she was just one of a quite common class of oreboats that were rapidly growing in their numbers on the lakes. But to Captain Massy she would soon become both home and office as he guided her up and down the lakes, her hold stuffed with coal upbound and ore downbound. There was always the autumn opportunity of hauling some late-season grain, but the *Mitchell* seemed to be at her best with coal or ore aboard. Such was the boat's lot and she took to her toil without a whimper each season.

Late in the first week of July 1911, the 4,468 ton *Mitchell* passed from Lake Erie and pounded up the Detroit River. In the boat's cargo hold was piled $35,000 worth of coal bound for Duluth. The vessel was working under the ownership of C.W. Elphicke of

Chicago and standing in command, as usual, was Captain Massy. Taking the better part of a whole day, the steamer snaked her way up the Detroit and St. Clair rivers. Another day was spent huffing up Lake Huron and into the St. Marys River, heading for the Soo. It was a trip that the *Mitchell* had made so often that Captain Massy felt that the crew could go ashore and the boat would somehow make the round trip on her own.

Warm and sticky was the air which hovered over Lake Erie and Lake Huron, a thick summer haze squeezing down upon the oreboats as they went about their work. Aboard the *John Mitchell* was one group of individuals who were particularly discomforted by July's dog-days. In their full-length, long sleeved white cotton dresses and matching summer hats, were six lady passengers, doing their best to cope with the heat, aided by tall glasses of iced tea and large hand-held fans. From the time they left Cleveland, Mrs. E.A. Smith, Mrs. A.A. Willcutt and Miss Clara Bundschuh, along with Mrs. William Grant, Mrs. Albert Grant and her daughter Alberta, had all sweltered in the smothering humidity. At least young William Grant, who was doing his best to play the part of the ladies' escort to the untamed north, could roll his sleeves up a bit or loosen his collar and still be socially proper. The ladies, however, were not permitted such displays of public laxity on even the hottest days of 1911.

At half past four on the lazy Sunday afternoon of July ninth, in the park adjacent to the locks at the Soo, people had spread elegant picnics upon the grass, as if the scurrying bustle of lake commerce did not exist around them. Quietly the giant steel hull of the *John Mitchell* pushed steadily into the lock, the only noise being that of the water seeping through the lock gates. The landing boom would not be invented for another year and a half, so onto the lock wall a pair of deckhands made their way via rope and ladder. The boat's lines in worn hands, the crewmen walked ahead of the steamer as if leading a plow horse. As the *Mitchell* entered the lock, the deckhands were joined by the lockmen and together they shouted commands and guided the oreboat into the lock, making her lines fast to the bits. Keeping well ahead of the steamer's motion, the captain already had her engine reversed and as she came to a near stop the deck crew got her steam winches clanking, to pull the boat the remaining way into the lock. The gates at the lower end of the lock slowly swung closed and the valves under the lock were opened, allowing the higher water above the lock to flow in underneath. The power of countless tons of lake water, bound to seek its own level, began slowly and steadily to lift the *Mitchell*. No pumps, no electricity, just the law of physics.

From the *Mitchell's* rail, the ladies from Cleveland watched with great curiosity, as the massive steamer was raised effortlessly beneath their feet. As the boat's spar deck rose to a point level with the lock wall, the deck hands stepped casually back aboard. For the ladies, the whole scene was a bit disorienting. The movement of the boat was nearly imperceptible, yet they began to notice that they were looking at their surroundings from a much higher angle. They felt no movement and the only sound was the syncopated clanks of the winches, as the ever-taut lines were let out to compensate for the rising hull. The guests' attention was shifted by young Clara Clemens, the cook's daughter, to the starboard side of the boat, where the rapids of the St. Marys River could be seen in the distance. Shooting down the cascades went a large canoe, with a man paddling each end and a half dozen shrieking tourists seated between. "They're Indians," Clara explained knowingly, "for a dollar they'll run you down the rapids." Watching the soaking that the thrilled canoers were being exposed to, the six proper ladies gasped gleefully and debated whether or not it was worth the price of a dollar.

All at once the entire group was startled, as a single short throaty blast from the *Mitchell's* steam whistle split their conversation. It was Captain Massy's signal to all that the boat was prepared to leave the locks. The lines leading aft to the bits on the lock wall were slackened by the steam winches and released by the lockmen. The lines leading forward were left to slack on their own, as the *Mitchell* began to inch forward out of the lock, when they too were released from the bits. Billowing a thick black cloud from her giant stack, the steamer began to pick up forward way and slide ahead. The deck winches clanked as steel lines were taken back aboard and with no more fanfare than that, the

John Mitchell steamed from the western mouth of the canal and on toward Lake Superior.

With a cool, refreshing breeze lofting in off Whitefish Bay, the weather had taken a noticeably pleasant turn. At long last, those aboard the *Mitchell* felt some relief from the repressive humidity. Shortly after the *Mitchell* left the Soo, cook Al Clemens rang the dinner bell and everyone not on duty gathered for another of his hearty meals. Aboard the *Mitchell*, each repast was a family affair with Al Clemens cooking, his wife serving and his daughter Clara helping where she could. Talk across the dinner table that Sunday evening was largely of the good sleeping weather that the coming night would bring and all around the boat the mood was as fresh as the gentle breeze that came across the lake.

That same cool breeze which brought a reprieve from the humidity, brought something else. As the sun set, the air grew dense with fog, and the breeze abruptly vanished. The *Mitchell* was surrounded by cotton fog so thick that the after cabins could not be seen from the pilothouse less than 400-feet away. Checking his speed, Captain Massy brought the *Mitchell* to a skulk. The boat and crew now became a surreal little world unto themselves… there was no radar, radio direction finder or marine radio telephone to break the steamer's isolation. These devices were so far in the future that Captain Massy could not even imagine such things. All he had was his compass and clock, and he was very adept at using them. At the current engine revolutions, he figured the boat's speed at just over three miles-per-hour, which would put him clear of Whitefish Point at 10 p.m. At that time he would turn to a 294-degree course, bringing him to nearly the center of the lake, some 28 miles abeam of Isle Royale at about sunset Monday. This calculation was based on the hope that the fog would break by dawn or that once on open Lake Superior, the *Mitchell* would just sail out from under the curtain. In either case, he could increase the revolutions to a good running speed and once again start making good time.

As Captain Massy and the crew groped blindly across Whitefish Bay, many other lakers hauled past them downbound, some seen, most only heard, for like the *Mitchell* the fog-shrouded downbounders had their whistles blowing-the standard signal for vessels moving in fog. The problem was that there were many vessels moving across the waters in the vicinity of Whitefish Bay that gray night. Sometimes the air would echo with distant and close whistles overlapping one another, then protracted moments of deep silence, followed by the random whistles once more.

This manner of "feeling" your way instinctively through the restricted waterways of the Great Lakes has long been a skill for which lake mariners have become famous. Salt water sailors who have always relied on volumes of charts, harbor pilots and teams of tugs to find their way, refer jokingly to their Great Lakes counterparts' methods as "dog barking." The implication is that every lakeboat has a dog on board and likewise every cabin near every bend along the waterways has a dog. Considering that every dog along the lakes, just like every mariner, supposedly knows one another, the captain of any boat needs only to put his dog at the bow and set that dog to barking, which starts every other dog barking. Now the captain can navigate and avoid other boats by the familiar barking. That is how tightly the Great Lakes sailing community is knitted.

Unfortunately for Captain Massy, the fallacy of "dog barkin" was nowhere near the truth. There were only the barks of distant steam whistles echoing in the mist. Camouflaged among the distant whistles were the throaty sobs from the whistle of the 376-foot steel oreboat *William Henry Mack*. In the distance the sound wavered and melted away in the fog. From the *Mack's* pilothouse window, Captain George H. Burnham was guiding the boat down toward the Soo in the employ of the Jenkins Steamship Company. Setting high out of the water, the *Mack* was making a rare downbound trip without cargo. Such trips obviously pay nothing, so vessel masters and owners alike were compelled to get them completed and put the next paying cargo aboard as soon as possible. Without doubt, Captain Burnham was motivated to "keep her comin" down the lake, and was pushing his speed as much as the boat's unburdened status would allow. The fog bank that he had run into at Superior's lower end presented an unwelcome delay, to say the least. Fog meant checking the engine's turns and in order to comply with the maritime regulations, Captain Burnham brought the

Mack's speed down from sprint to fast walk. Considering the thick conditions this was a token effort at best.

Just before midnight, destiny brought the *William Henry Mack* and the *John Mitchell* together. Like his counterpart aboard the *Mitchell*, Captain Burnham had seen the lights appear ahead of the *Mack's* steering pole an instant before the two oreboats collided. Instinctively, he grabbed the engine telegraph and rang reverse, but before an acknowledgement from the chief could ring back, the two monsters slammed together. So great had been the *Mack's* forward speed that the impact tossed sleeping crewmen from their bunks. This was no demonstration of prudent checking of revolutions for the current weather conditions.

Most of the *Mitchell's* crew, as well as the passengers from Cleveland, were sound asleep when the steamers came crashing into one another. The ladies staggered from their rooms, rubbing their eyes, still half asleep. Reaching the deck, Mrs. Grant found the fog so thick it was nearly impossible to find her way around. From every direction in the dense mist, the shouts echoed and were intermixed with deep groans from twisting hull plates. Shadows of crew members dashed about urgently, their familiar faces obscured by the fog. Somehow, Mrs. Grant was the last of her group to reach the deck, and was now separated from the rest. From the stern she heard the voice of Captain Massy, urging everyone aft, and she set out stumbling across the deck toward the lifeboat stations atop the stern deck house, clad only in her nightclothes.

Emerging from the Clemens family quarters, young Clara knew just by the tilt of the deck and the frantic actions of the crew that the *Mitchell* was sinking. Before she had a chance to be afraid, she was swept up by her parents as the whole family made for the boat deck. As the family hovered near the lifeboat, they could see the crew, who were not working at the lifeboats, had strung a few lines between the *Mitchell* and the *Mack*. To Clara it must have seemed silly that they were attempting to keep the *Mitchell* afloat by using a few skimpy ropes. In actuality, the lines had been rigged as a standby, in the event the steamer suddenly started to go down before the yawls could be swung out. It was hoped that at least some of the crew could scramble across to safety. If this would have worked or not is debatable, but just the effort of rigging the lines must have been a comfort.

A hole large enough to drive a truck through had been punched into the *Mitchell's* starboard side, just forward of mid-ship about one third of the way back from the bow. Lake Superior was now cascading into the cargo hold, as if the boat were a thirsty steel monster. The collision with the *Mack* had inflicted a mortal wound that no power on earth could heal... the *Mitchell* was doomed. Her own inertia had already torn the *Mack* loose from the *Mitchell* and she was now drifting alongside, her bow ripped open and yawning up to the eight foot mark.

Clara Clemens, with her parents and two crewmen, was placed into one of two lifeboats that had always waited atop the aft deck house. As the boat was being swung out, Al Clemens mumbled something about "the jewelry," bounded from the yawl and stumbled his way into the mist. A moment later the *Mitchell* lurched, jarring the lines loose that held the lifeboat. The yawl slammed hard onto the steel deck, so hard in fact, that the impact fractured the leg of Clara's mother. In an instant, the lifeboat tumbled over the side, dumping all aboard 20 odd feet into Lake Superior's frigid soup.

As she came to the surface, young Clara found the yawl floating bottom side up and all of the others clinging to its keel. The two crewmen began thrashing wildly with their feet and uttering loud grunts as they wrestled to flip the lifeboat back over. Quickly taking account of the situation, Clara knew that if something did not change in a hurry some, or perhaps all of those in the water would soon tire and perish in the cold lake. This was especially true of her mother who, suffering with a broken leg, was on the verge of unconsciousness and barely able to keep her head above water. Gazing up the towering steel side of the *Mack*, she spied several of the crew standing at the rail, feeling utterly helpless. Thinking fast, the plucky young lady conceived a plan and shouted up to the *Mack's* crew to throw down a line. Instantly the men began scrambling over one another and a moment later one of them appeared at the rail with a thick rope. With a splash the line came slapping down just within Clara's reach, she wasted not a moment in fastening it to the capsized yawl. With the crew of the *Mack* tugging on the far end and those in the water thrashing and grunting once more, the lifeboat flipped upright and the drenched castaways were dragged safely aboard the yawl. As Mrs. Clemens was pulled from the lake, she fainted from exhaustion.

While Clara Clemens' ordeal was being played out down on the lake's surface, Mrs. Grant had managed to fumble her way to the stern, where the crew was gathered around one of the long rung ladders that had been bridged across to the *Mack*. At the urging of the *Mitchell's* crew, the ladies were sent crawling across to the *Mack*. Unceremoniously, Mrs. Grant was hustled onto the wobbling wooden ladder and with baboon-like posture, began making her way to the *Mack*. The water was barely visible more than two stories below in the fog and as each of her hands and knees clunked onto the rungs of the ladder, she was sure that at any moment she would surely topple over and be consumed by the misty darkness below. Behind her the death groans of the *Mitchell* echoed like a stalking giant and the frantic crew followed as if pursued. She had no time for terror, she felt as if her heart no longer beat, she just closed her eyes and kept crawling hand-and-knee. Suddenly, what felt like a dozen warm burly hands reached out and snatched her from the teetering nightmare. Mrs. Grant was aboard the *Mack*, safe from the foundering *Mitchell*. Right behind her scrambled a traffic jam of crewmen and

Seen here in better times, the 440-foot John Mitchell now rests upside down and imbedded into the mud on Lake Superior's bottom. She is the permanent tomb of her cook who lost his life in an attempt to save his family jewelry.

just as the last of them stepped to safety, the *Mitchell* lurched violently, snapping the lines to the *Mack* like threads and rolled over and plunged to the bottom in a hissing whirlpool that turned suddenly into a boiling hill of icy black water.

Hand over hand, the *Mack's* crew dragged at the rope still attached to the swamped yawl boat, with the remainder of the Clemens family. As they were brought aboard the *Mack*, young Clara found that her father was not among the survivors clamoring on the deck and her courage gave way to shock, as she fainted into unconsciousness. The oblivious Clemens ladies, along with all the other ladies, were escorted to the captain's cabin where they remained, as the *Mack* limped to the Soo.

Sunrise the following morning saw the wounded *Mack* tied up to the Government Pier at the American Soo, her bow slashed open in a shark-like grin, just above the waterline. All about the decks was scattered the litter of disaster. Jumbles of rope, ladders and lifeboats gave mute account of what had transpired in the cotton fog off Whitefish Point. When the *Mitchell* died she took only three of her crew with her: Second Mate Archie Causley, Watchman George Austin and Cook Al Clemens. That fact alone said much about the brave work of all who had been involved. The weeks and years ahead would see certificate action against both masters, along with finger-pointing and the usual claims against both shipping companies. All this a result of one night, when the dogs just were not barkin'.

The wreck rests today upside down in 150-feet of water, her cabins crushed into the muddy bottom by the weight of the massive hull. It is a haunting display in Lake Superior's ice water museum, where Al Clemens traded his life to become permanent custodian of a few jewels... forever entombed in the overturned hull of the *John Mitchell*.

HOURIGAN'S QUESTION

As John Hourigan clung to the telephone pole sized, ice-coated mast with the angry lake roaring below him and seething with wreckage, only one thought kept running through his mind, "Shall I ever see my children again?" As the hours dragged on, his question became a plea and soon a prayer. Too numb from the cold to even shiver any longer, he prayed, he shouted for help and he held on with all of his soul. The night had turned so black that he often felt blind. There were no stars or moon showing through the storm clouds and no lights in the distance. Hourigan could not even see his shipmate, Edward J. Igoe, clinging to the same perch just a few feet above him. His entire universe was the groaning mast, the howling wind, the spitting snow from the blizzard and the odds were that neither of these two mariners would live to see the daylight of the next day. Over the decades, countless other mariners had been lost to the lakes while clinging to a mast as their vessel slowly went to pieces beneath them. So it was that the answer to Hourigan's question may just be, "No, you will not see your children again;" it was the end of the shipping season of 1873.

Events taking place were very different six and one half years earlier on a fine spring day in Sacket's Harbor, New York. Located at the eastern most tip of Lake Ontario, the finest of spring weather was now hovering over the port city. The day was much like a holiday with the Adams Center band playing festive music and a lively game of baseball taking place at the town's local field. Dressed in their finest springtime apparel the local folks strolled about and socialized. Parasols and floppy hats adorned the ladies while gentlemen sported felt hats and starched collars. The event that was creating such a holiday atmosphere was the launching of a new Great Lakes vessel, the schooner *Wm. B. Phelps*. Measuring "canaller size" at 137-feet long and 26-feet in beam, the new boat would have an 11-foot depth and weigh in at 297 gross tons, exactly that needed to transition the Welland Canal. She had been built to run the coasts of Lake Ontario and navigate the waters of the mouth of the St. Lawrence River. Sporting three tall masts and having a retractable centerboard she was a thing of beauty and the side launching was sure to be a spectacular event. The boat was being named in honor of William B. Phelps who was the Superintendent of the Oswego and Syracuse Railroad. Contracts for the construction were placed with the shipyard of B. Eveleigh by John Dunn &

Company of Oswego, New York. The actual building of the schooner was started in September of 1872 under the watchful supervision of the boat's first captain, William Carter. Thus this festive spring scene was capped off with the spectacle of the newly christened *Phelps* splashing into the water among the cheers of hundreds of local folks. Tours that day showed that she was well equipped and had spacious accommodations for a schooner of her day. Her cabin was "neatly arranged" with a large dining room and galley. She had been designed with state rooms, a "wash room" and even a parlor for her captain. On her deck was a Tallcott patent capstan cast by Middlebrook & Mack of Oswego. On the Wednesday following her launching, the *Phelps* headed out on her maiden voyage which would take her to Oswego to pick up a cargo of salt bound through the canal to Chicago.

After a half dozen seasons of sailing the Great Lakes, the *Phelps* was still considered practically a new boat as she was making a late season run across the lakes. It was, perhaps, that like-new condition that inspired her owners to send her to the western lakes in the last two weeks of November, 1879. It was a risky move just for some 18,000 bushels of wheat and 600 cases of beer. Her captain in 1879 was Dan Kelly, an Oswego resident who had aboard his kin, George Kelley. Records as to their family relationship have yet to be uncovered although George has been described in local newspapers as being "a boy" and may well have been the captain's son. Also on the crew were First Mate

John Hourigan and crewmen Frank Robert Downey, Edward J. Igoe and one man who never had his name recorded. This crew sailed the *Phelps* into the worst part of the year on the lakes. A series of strong gales had swept the freshwater seas since mid-November and on the 19th day of that month the *Phelps* found herself in the teeth of the worst of that weather.

Pounding her way in the northeast corner of Lake Michigan, the *Phelps* began losing her fight with the wind and waves at mid-day. By evening the winds from the northwest had blown out her storm sails and the frigid spray from the waves had coated her decks with ice. Those spacious cabins below her decks were now flooded with waste-deep sloshing ice water. So thick was the ice on her decks that her crew could not venture out to service any of her apparatus. Any foot that was set onto the water-slicked ice would immediately slip off and the person attached to it would simply slide into the lake's deadly grasp. The people of the *Phelps* could do nothing more than hold on and wait to meet their fate.

Just after 7 o'clock on the evening of November 19th, 1879 the schooner *Wm. B. Phelps* went from active sailing vessel to shipwreck as she was driven stern-first into the sandy shallows just 60 yards off of the Michigan shoreline. Her crew had not been able to retract the boat's centerboard and as her bulk was forced into the sand the centerboard was shoved up through the decks as the *Phelps* cracked like an egg amidships. The hull telescoped upon itself and the entire mid-section and stern of the boat began to quickly break up. Her crew scrambled to save themselves in any manner that they could think of. Breaking waves immediately began exploding over the boat like giant ice water fists. Some of her crew were simply washed away right then and there, while others continued to struggle. The area that had once been her decks now turned into a jumble of storm-tossed wreckage heaving with each wave. Deck timbers, masts, sails and furniture were mixed in a web of ropes and rigging. The only part of the vessel left in one piece was a portion of the bow and the decking which supported the forward mast. It was there that John Hourigan, Edward Igoe and young Robert Downey took refuge by climbing the mast and literally holding on for their lives.

Soon after the trio of survivors had scaled the mast to escape the waves, the youthful Downey spotted a piece of deck floating like a raft at the end of one of the *Phelps'* fallen spars. He shouted to the others that he thought he could get to it and free it up so as to float his way to shore. In fact they all thought that the piece of decking could support all three of them for a ride to dry land. Downey decided to go first and free the makeshift raft, drag it over closer to Hourigan and Igoe and then they could all float free. As the two men still on the mast watched, Downey made his way through the gale along the spar. Against all odds he reached the piece of deck and managed to jump onto it. He managed to get the piece to float free for a short time before the winds and swirling seas drove it directly into the tangled mass of debris hanging off of the leeward side of the wreck. There both the makeshift raft and Downey became hopelessly ensnared. With no way to cross the debris field and return to the safe haven of the mast where his shipmates were perched, Downey found himself stranded on a tiny island of frozen death. As the darkness grew, Hourigan and Igoe could soon make out only the faintest image of Downey in the bitter cold stormy night. They yelled encouragements to him, but after a while he just laid down on his little raft. Soon his voice simply stopped coming back from the blackness, he had frozen to death.

Daylight came grudgingly and revealed that Hourigan and Igoe were both still alive. Too benumbed to move, the two men were simply waiting for their mast to fall and Lake Michigan to claim them as it had their shipmates. Each wave swayed the mast and only the ice that had formed on the wreck was holding their safe haven together. Each oncoming wave threatened to sweep the wreck clean and erase their lives.

It was then that a local resident of Glen Arbor, Michigan, a tiny village located just a mile west of the wreck; came walking along the beach and discovered their plight. Modern research has yet to uncover the name of that beach combing person and the persons identity may indeed be lost to history, but what that person did was what any good citizen would likely do, which was to run to town and sound the alarm of "Shipwreck!" The townspeople of Glen Arbor were soon mustered on the beach adjacent to the remains of the *Phelps*. At a glance everyone knew that the two survivors could not last much longer in the cold and a hasty plan to rescue them was devised. Using a leaky old flat-bottomed fish-boat, five of the locals set out across the churning field of wreckage to save the two stranded mariners. William A. Clark, Charles A. Rosman, John Tobin, Welby C. Ray and William Tucker launched the fish-boat into the surf and clamored aboard. The five would-be heroes never even reached the wreckage field as the winds and surf easily thwarted their effort. Pulling the flooded fish-boat and the five drenched rescuers back ashore, the town's people quickly formulated a better version of their rescue plan. They dragged the fish-boat 330-feet upwind of the wreck and launched it again. This time, they figured to let the winds work for them rather than against them. William Tucker's place in the fish-boat was taken by Howard Daniels as the rescuers set out once again. Encouraged by the cries from the two stranded crewmen, the five man rescue team this time managed to reach the stern of the wreck and attach a line to it. There they sat as the folly of their hasty rescue effort suddenly became clear. The two stranded mariners were at the bow of the *Phelps*, while the fish-boat was at the stern. The windward side of the wreck was peppered with the onslaught of exploding surf that would easily sink the fish-boat. The leeward side of the wreck was a huge churning mass of jagged wreckage mixed with an icy web of rigging that was equally impassable. The rescue party may as well have been on the beach for all the good that their current position would do. Soaked, cold and ice-covered, they had no choice other than to retreat back to the shore and consider another plan.

By the time that the rescue party reached the sands of dry land, they were exhausted and benumbed by the frigid lake. It was decided that they should all return home, put on dry clothing more suitable for fighting off the wind and waves and come back immediately to continue the struggle. Leaving a party on the beach, so that the stranded mariners would not think that they had been deserted, the rescuers ran to their homes, changed from their frozen clothing and returned to again try and rob Lake Michigan of two poor souls. By the time they reached the beach the crowd of local residents had grown in number. It seemed as if every person in the village of Glen Arbor was now there to witness the drama. This time the plan was to challenge the mass of wreckage between the rescue fish-boat and the wreck of the *Phelps*. The boat's flat bottom, it was reasoned, could be used to ride up upon the wreckage and perhaps maneuver close enough to get a line tossed to the two shipwrecked sailors. This time rescuer Howard Daniels was replaced in the party by John Blanchfield as the fish-boat departed once again. To say that the trip was hazardous would be much more than an understatement. The water was cold enough to suck the life out of any man in a matter minutes, the waves were bursting over the wreck every few seconds with their spray quickly turning to ice and the layers of

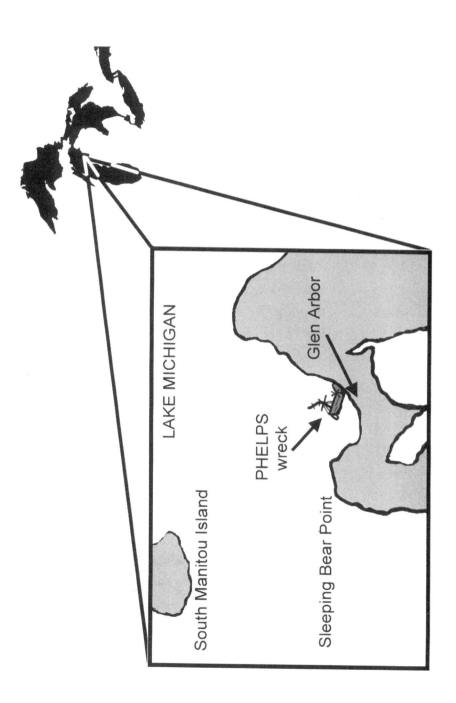

clothing that each rescuer wore would soak up enough water to drag them down in an instant should they be tossed into the lake. To make the matter worse, huge pieces of the wreck were heaving upon the waters and constantly threatening to hammer the little fish-boat to the bottom. But the rescuers were encouraged on by the repeated cry of those men that they had set out to save. From the wreck came the voice, hardly audible over the howling wind, "Pull hard boys! Pull hard!"

Somehow the sting of the cold and the threat of the wreckage no longer mattered to the five rescuers. Only those words and their plea to "Pull hard, pull hard!" mattered as the tiny fish-boat was directed against the odds and against the elements toward the stranded souls beyond. Finally the little boat was driven into the wreckage and wedged in place about 60-feet from the stranded mariners. Time was short as each undulation of the heaving wreckage field threatened to smash the tiny craft. In a single toss a line was thrown to John Hourigan. Somehow his benumbed hands managed to keep a hold on the line which he quickly fastened around himself. With that single line being the thread on which his life itself dangled, Hourigan left his perch to begin the dangerous trek across the wreckage toward the fish-boat. He could not feel his feet or his legs and only his instinct to survive kept him from toppling into the deadly waters below. Crawling over the wreckage Hourigan managed to get within fifteen feet of the fish-boat and onto a large piece of the *Phelps'* deck where he finally ran out of strength and lay down as if to die.

The rescue crew pulled their fish-boat over to that piece of deck and heaved the little flat-bottom boat onto it. They then reached out and their hands plucked Hourigan from death.

Following behind Hourigan came Edward Igoe, but his condition was far worse than Hourigan. Suffering from hypothermia, Igoe was weakened to the point of resignation, and when his foot became wedged into the wreckage he was only able to feebly struggle. Seeing that they were about to lose poor Igoe, two of the rescuers jumped from the boat and hopped from one piece of wreckage to another until they got to him. They promptly freed his leg and then dragged him by the collar of his shirt along a floating spar until they reached the same piece of deck upon which Hourigan had collapsed. From there the rest of the party pulled everyone into the fish-boat and a rapid retreat toward the beach was made.

Just a few yards from dry land the overburdened fish-boat began to fill with frigid Lake Michigan and sink. For a moment it appeared as if the rescue effort had been baited into a death trap that would now claim all seven men. Seeing this, nearly the entire town of Glen Arbor at once summoned a determination to fight the lake and the gale. In a single charge the crowd stormed the surf and rescued the rescuers. As a community, they saved the day and the lives of seven brave men. As Hourigan stepped upon the beach he raised his arms and in a tearful sob cried "Thank God! I shall see children again!" In the arms of the residents of Glen Arbor the two helpless survivors of the wreck of the *Phelps* were taken to the local hotel about a mile from the wreck site. There they were tended to by the community for the next week as they recovered sufficiently to make their way home. Hourigan's prayer was indeed answered as he did see his beloved children again. Of all of the lost crew of the *Phelps*, only young Daniel Downey's body was ever recovered. The rest of the crew were swallowed by Lake Michigan and buried in her sands as is the *Phelps* herself, they all remain there to this day.

TRIP 29

For the better part of a full day and night, the two marine legs from Buffalo, New York's Standard Grain dock's elevators have been stretched into the open hatches of the Interlake Steamship Company's 647-foot steamer *J.L. Mauthe*. Hungrily, the belted clamshells that run the length of each leg, are chewing away at the boat's cargo of grain. Normally, this system could devour about 13,000 bushes per hour, but today the apparatus is running a bit slow at about 9,000 bushels per hour. It is dawn on Saturday, the fifth day of December 1992 and the *Mauthe* and her crew are engaged in the annual tradition of hauling as much late-season grain as possible from the upper lakes, before Arctic winds turn the freshwater seas to solid ice.

Buffalo has long been one of the major grain terminals on the Great Lakes, much longer than most people would think. The first trickles of grain came into the port just before 1830. Within the next six years the business boomed, fed by the expanding farmlands to the west. By 1841, Buffalo harbor was a veritable forest of masts, attached to sailing vessels that had come east burdened with grain. The difficulty was the unloading method of the day, slow enough to make a snail's crawl appear swift. Block and tackle were used to lower baskets through the boat hatches, where the grain was shoveled in by hand and hoisted to a 10 to 15 bushel hopper and scale, suspended above. Weighed, it was bagged or barreled and carried ashore by immigrant laborers. To complicate this process, work must be halted each time rain fell or storm winds kicked up. Only 1,800 to 2,000 bushels could go ashore in a full day. Comparatively, at that same rate, in modern times, it would take 345 days, or nearly 11 and one half months, to unload one cargo carried by the *J.L. Mauthe*.

Fortunately for the crew of the *Mauthe*, as well as the Interlake Steamship Company, a Buffalo businessman named Joseph Dart had a better idea in 1841. Borrowing a Revolutionary War era concept for milling grain, developed by Oliver Evans and called the "hopper-boy," Dart attached a series of two-quart capacity buckets 28 inches apart on a continuous leather belt. The whole rig was attached to a long leg that could be extended directly from the elevator to a boat's cargo hold. A steam engine ran the whole contraption. Many around Buffalo scoffed at the device, after all "Irishmen's backs," according to Dart's close friend Mahlon Kingsman, "are the cheapest elevators ever built." The critics were abruptly silenced when the schooner *John S. Skinner*, with 4,000 bushels aboard, was unloaded in just four hours proving Dart's belt-and-buckets were a marvel. Later, the buckets were enlarged and spaced closer on the belt. Additionally, longshoremen or "scoopers" wielding giant wooden dustpan-like trays propelled by ropes driven off of the legs, were used to pile the tail ends of cargos at the buckets. By the 1860s, capacity was up to 7,000 bushels per hour. In the afternoon of December 5th, 1992, swirling snow squalls, mixed with grain dust, surround the *J.L. Mauthe* as "scoopers" sling the last of her cargo toward the legs. No one remembers Joseph Dart, who invented the unloading gear they are using, which shortens the big steamer's dock time by 11 and one-half months and put thousands of immigrants out of work.

Throughout the *Mauthe's* unloading, an early winter gale had been sweeping across Lake Erie and dumping lake-effect snow from the Buffalo shore inland. Shuffling about in the pilothouse as the last grain went up the legs, is relief master, Captain Bryon "easy does it" Petz. Perusing the latest weather-fax, Captain Petz figures that the slightly lower rate of the unloading rigs will work in the *Mauthe's* favor. The gales would be diminishing through the day and the evening winds should turn to a bluster. Lake Erie, the shallowest of the Great Lakes, has a distinct tendency to become quickly enraged at the first taste of storm winds, but to die down just as rapidly when the winds subside. The *Mauthe's* delay in unloading ought to allow just enough time for the lake to settle down.

In a blizzard, the dart's legs chew away at the J.L. Mauthe's *grain cargo in Buffalo. Author's photo*

As the scoopers finished their dusty toil, the *Mauthe's* captain has two concerns on his mind that carry a far greater urgency than temperamental Lake Erie. A second storm system is, at the moment, upsetting Lake Superior. "There's a low passin' Superior at 29 even..." the captain informs Third Mate Doug Cooley, who is climbing the stairs to the pilothouse. The master's reference is to the barometric pressure being measured at 29.00 inches of mercury. 29.92 is considered standard and the lower the pressure the stronger the storm. "The lowest I ever saw it was 28.80," the master continues, with his attention drawn out across the *Mauthe's* stern. Directly behind the steamer is the brooding black iron girders of the Ohio Street aerial lift bridge. It is the gateway to the tightest, and by all considerations, the worst turn on the Great Lakes. Gales and ice the lake mariners take in stride, but the Ohio Street turn has kept many a captain awake at night. When the *Mauthe* is empty, Captain Petz must back his boat through Ohio Street, with the aid of a single tug.

While the Dart marine legs are lifted from the now-empty hold, deckhands secure the last of the *Mauthe's* giant steel hatch covers. Each hatch cover is a single plate, held in place by a series of clamps. Movement of the hatch covers requires the use of a deck-mounted crane, running the length of the spar deck on rails. Use of this "iron deckhand" makes placing the hatches a two-man job, at best. The last clamp snapped in place, the "G" tug *Iowa* hovers near the stern and lines are passed. In the pilothouse comes a pop and a hiss as the captain fires up the bow thruster. "Don't let this powerful thing throw ya' off your feet now," he quips to the wheelsman. The *Mauthe's* bow thruster is a bit underpowered and keeps captains on their toes especially at Ohio Street.

Like watching a clock run, the process of wiggling a 647-foot steamer through Ohio Street is worse than slow. With only a bit of ballast in her forward tanks to keep the bow thruster effective, the *Mauthe* is slightly head down but riding about as high out of the water as she can. "We don't want any wind now," the master murmurs as the bow comes clear of the dock and the bridge begins to lift. On deck all three mates call out distances in a team effort to overcome Ohio Street.

Over channel 10 the first mate's voice crackles, "Closest point on the port quarter is about 36-feet off the wall, 36." The radio chatter reverberates through the pilothouse, the bridge footings vanish from view below the bow rail and the captain and wheelsman must rely on the third mate, leaning over the side, to be their eyes. "Eight feet off these pilings on the fore-bow!" he calls and after a long silence, "10-feet off the fore-bow," is transmitted in a more subdued tone. "That's it Doug, just keep talkin'," answers the captain. From deep below, the bow thruster rumbled and aft the tug *Iowa* zigzags with the towline. The Ohio Street pavement stretches out toward the hull, "and we're reachin' out toward the center of the next stretch," the first mate finally calls from astern, "you got daylight on that starboard side," comes from the bow. "Call 'em and tell 'em put 20-feet in two through six and let me know when it's in, Tom," the captain directs the wheelsman. The *Mauthe* is clear of the bridge and needed ballast can now be pumped aboard. "20-feet two through six," the wheelsman echoes, cranking the bell on the engine room phone. The *J.L. Mauthe* and crew have defeated Ohio Street again.

Interestingly, the crew of the *Mauthe* make this turn with regularity, completely unaware of the melee that occurred there the night of January 21, 1959. It is a story that may just make them regard the Ohio Street turn in a different light. On that bitter Thursday night in 1959, the Kinsman Transit Company's 440-foot steamer *Mac Gilvray Shiras* was sleeping in winter lay-up at the

Concrete-Central Elevator at the upper end of Buffalo Creek. Downstream from the *Shiras* a dozen lakers also were hibernating at winter quarters along the river bank. This fleet included the 545-foot steamer *Michael K. Tewksbury*, moored at the Standard Elevator from which the *Mauthe* would take cargos 33 years later. With a gale blowing and ice floes wedged against her hull, the *Shiras* began parting her mooring lines just after 10 o'clock in the evening and by 10:40 her massive hull was drifting downstream, driven by the wind. There was no crew manning the *Shiras*, just her flustered ship keeper aboard. In an effort to stop the *Shiras'* drift, the shipkeeper released the anchors. Unfortunately, he had neglected to clear the "devil's claws" (used to keep the anchors from accidentally dropping), so the big chains became hopelessly jammed.

Miraculously, the *Shiras* drifted right down the center of the stream, sliding cleanly past every boat until she reached the Standard Elevator and the *Michael K. Tewksbury*. As the *Shiras* rounded the bend above the Standard Elevator, she could not fit between the *Tewksbury* and the *B.W. Druckenmiller*, in lay-up across the river. With a loud thump, the *Shiras* slammed stern-first into the *Tewksbury's* bow, forcing that boat to part her lines and similarly go adrift. At that moment, the two wayward lakeboats proceeded to do the impossible, together. Without aid of tugs, rudders, engine power or even crews, they slipped through Ohio Street, made the turn and continued downstream. The entire rampage ended 37 minutes after it began, when the boats piled into the Michigan Avenue bridge. If the crew of the *Mauthe* knew of this remarkable event, they would doubtless regard their present chore in a slightly different way.

After nearly two hours, the *Mauthe* is clear of Buffalo Creek, poised behind the breakwater. The tug *Iowa* is set free and using a hard-over rudder and the bow thruster the big steamer is pivoted nearly 180 degrees to point toward an ink-black Lake Erie. The chadburn rings to full ahead and the captain calls down to the engine room to order the lake-gate. Distancing from the breakwater, the *Mauthe* begins her familiar wobble, caused by one slightly-dinged propeller blade. The steering apparatus is set to "auto" and the superb steel steamer heads toward Long Point.

The auto-pilot is holding the wheel, but that by no means implies the pilothouse is vacated. A watch is kept from the windows constantly, for while the boat is moving, barely a second passes that at least one pair of eyes is not scrutinizing the distance. Both the *Mauthe* radars keep an unending watch, beyond the point that the human eye can see. All that is visible in the distance this night is a single dim light on the far horizon ahead. The radar reveals a target, but the *Mauthe* is closing at a rate of less than one mile each hour, so it will be dawn before the other upbounder will be close enough to deal with. Lake Erie had calmed to a dead swell. The captain turns the pilothouse over to the third mate as the *Mauthe* steams into the night and the lights of Buffalo begin to fade astern. Trip number 29 has begun.

With the beginning of Trip 29 on this cold day in 1992, this big steamer holds the position of being the smallest member of the immaculate fleet of lakeboats that comprise the Interlake Steamship Company. In an era that has seen many once powerful U.S. Great Lakes fleets fade into history or become a small division of some distant corporation, the historic Interlake fleet has stood against the hard times, enduring as the lakes themselves. While other fleets appear on the edge, Interlake sports four 1000-footers or "footers" as the mariners call them. Formed in 1913, the company today has 11 bottoms with a combined single-trip carrying capacity of 389,567 tons. Interestingly, the 1948 Ship Masters Association Directory lists Interlake's single-trip fleet capacity at 364,900 tons, but that is using 36 vessels. Much has changed over the years, but one characteristic remains the same, Interlake has the character of a small local business where everyone, from deckhand to executive, is as down-to-earth friendly as the corner shopkeeper of 1948.

When she came out of the Great Lakes Engineering Works River Rouge yard in 1953, the *J.L. Mauthe* was hull number 298. Measuring 70-feet across her beam and 36-feet in depth, the *Mauthe* was one of a half dozen nearly identical oreboats. The six boats were dubbed the AAAs or "Pittsburgh class," since half of them, the *Arthur M. Anderson*, *Cason J. Callaway* and *Philip R. Clarke*, had gone to the once dominant Pittsburgh Steamship Company. The remaining boats, *William Clay Ford* and *Reserve*, went to the Ford

Motor Company and the Columbia Transportation Company, respectively. One trait set the *Mauthe* apart to the casual boat watcher, the after cabins were one deck house shy of her sisters, giving her a slightly submarine-decker appearance.

A colorful December sunrise cracked through the clouds the next morning, lasting long enough to brighten the *Mauthe's* pilothouse as she beat her way across Lake Erie near the Southeast Shoal light. About three miles ahead, the salty *Lake Tahoe* turned out to be the light the *Mauthe* had been closing on through the night. As the two boats came into the zigzag channel that is Pelee Passage, the *Mauthe* took her place in the salty's wake for the trip up the Detroit and St. Clair rivers, while ahead, some downbounders are tracking through that same channel. It is a real bottleneck.

In the distance to the south, the tin-stacker *Cason J. Callaway* pushes over the horizon and within the hour slides in line, upbound, three miles behind the *Mauthe*. The marching order for the passage up appears to be the *Lake Tahoe*, the *J.L. Mauthe* and the *Cason J. Callaway*, all with scarcely three miles between them.

Some seven miles below the Detroit River light, the *Mauthe* is hauled around into the channel that will bring her into the lower Detroit River. At the same time the *Callaway* appears to depart her course and angle away on a sharp northwest track. The *Mauthe's* pilothouse binoculars show the *Callaway* taking spray over her bow-rail and down her fence, while the *Mauthe* has taken none at all. What is going on becomes clear: the

Callaway is cutting the corner running the shallows to buoys 13 and 14 in an effort to cut in front of the *Mauthe*, which is already in the channel. In the *Mauthe's* pilothouse, the consensus is that the *Callaway* is set on taking fuel at the Shell dock in Sarnia and by cutting in front of the *Mauthe*, she can save the two hours and force the delay onto the *J.L. Mauthe*. This may seem like a matter of little concern, but when you calculate the more than $1,000 per hour cost of running a big laker, it is a gamble that some are willing to take. Knowing that the *Callaway* has a stainless steel screw and that the *Mauthe* has a less efficient bronze screw, the *Callaway's* master is betting that his boat can cut the corner and beat the *Mauthe* into the single lane of upbound traffic in the Detroit River. But there is one hitch. The geometry does not work this time and all that has been accomplished is that the *Callaway* is now on a collision course with the *Mauthe*.

With the *Mauthe* running her course, the tin-stacker bores closer at about a 45 degree angle to the *Mauthe's* beam and less than 300 yards away, so the Interlake boat has been forced into a real dilemma. If Captain Petz checks the *Mauthe's* speed and at the same time the *Callaway* realizes the futility of its short-cut and tucks in astern, the big self-unloader will run up the Interlake boat's fantail. On the other hand, with the *Mauthe* running on the lake-gate, she has about as much speed as she can muster. If the *Callaway* does manage to squeeze in ahead, when she turns onto the channel course she will lose forward way and the

This sequence of video screen-captures shows the Cason J. Calloway *as she cuts into the Detroit River Channel, narrowly avoiding both the Detroit entrance marker (arrow) and the* J.L. Mauthe. *From Author's Video*

Mauthe will be forced into some heavy backing to avoid hitting her. Furthermore, if the *Callaway's* steering equipment should fail now, she will most certainly ram the *Mauthe* broadside, perhaps sending both boats to the bottom. All that the *Mauthe's* crew can do is squeeze as far into the downbound lane as possible and stand watching as the 767-foot *Cason J. Callaway* charges directly at them. With an expletive, veteran mariner Wally Watkins who is working as watchman in the *Mauthe's* pilothouse says aloud "...where are the survival suits!"

Angling between the buoy and the *Mauthe*, the *Callaway* draws to within a few hundred feet of the Interlake oreboat. With only a boat-width of space between the vessels, the *Callaway* enters the channel, hauling her rudder hard over and churning mud from the lake bottom. Deciding he wants no part of this, the *Mauthe's* master rings to check the boat's speed, but the laws of physics are not that easily cheated. The flow of water between the two massive hulls has created a venturi effect and the *Mauthe* is being pulled along with the *Callaway*. The captain rings down for 70 turns on the *Mauthe's* big screw and gradually the *Callaway* slowly pulls ahead. "This ain't the place to be racin'," the captain grumbles to the wheelsman, "he wants it, let 'em have it." The master will take third in line and a delay at the fuel dock if it means finishing the trip without having to rely on the survival suits to do so.

Oddly it is this sort of brinksmanship that often keeps masters of vessels in their commands. Although

Sulking at the lock wall on June 26, 1993, the Cason J. Callaway *shows no regrets at having once conflicted with the* J.L. Mauthe. *In an industry where hours are valued in thousands of dollars, such conflicts are a part of the business.*

reckless in nature, the corner cut by the *Callaway* probably equated to a savings to the company of more than $3,000 at about the same cost to the *Mauthe's* owners. Although it did not cost the *Callaway's* owners their vessel, largely due to the prudent actions of the *Mauthe's* master, it easily could have. At the end of the season, however, when the books are balanced in the front office, those who count the beans will be far away from the Detroit River channel and the possibility of being tossed into the deadly ice water. All they will see on the *Callaway's* record for this day will be no hint of delay. On the other hand, the *Mauthe's* record will show more than two hours of delay in her run up the river. That delay will fall directly on the captain. When the time for issuing command assignments comes next season, those two hours will indeed count. Thus the master who was reckless is thereby more likely to retain his command as opposed to the one who thought of the safety of his vessel first. It is the way things have always worked at every transportation company and it will never change.

Navigating the Detroit and St. Clair rivers, like all of the connecting waterways on the Great Lakes, is a unique process. Proper charts are pulled from their drawer and laid out on the table, but rarely used. The mariners who peer from the center windows of lakeboats no matter if they are third, second, first mates or captains, know these waterways so well that the turns, headings and landmarks are ingrained in their souls. Today the *Mauthe* will be brought up the lower Detroit River by Second Mate Jeff Green, a veteran of the lakes since 1967 and at the end of his fourth season on the *Mauthe*. Standing at the wheel behind the mate is Wheelsman Gary Myjak, who started on the lakes in 1966 and has steadied the *Mauthe's* wheel for 17 years. To say these mariners are experienced would be an understatement in the extreme.

"Just left her easy to that smokestack, that tall one with the smoke comin' out there," the mate directs casually and Myjak nimbly manipulates the wheel, as if the boat were a part of him. That is how it is done. Just as a good chess player can call moves from across the room because the whole board is pictured in his mind, the lake mariner calls each turn with the whole river pictured in his mind. Not only is the proper landmark important, but the speed that the point of the steering pole appears to move from one landmark to another, is essential. The mariner can discern when a turn is coming around too slow or too fast, whereas an untrained observer can see no difference. "Now bring her onto that apartment building and that should give you 74," the mate continues. "On the apartment building," the wheelsman echoes, as the compass repeater clicks to 074 degrees, "74." Selected at the right spot, the proper landmark gives the right heading. Even the rate that the wheelsman hears the repeater click is used in judging the turns.

In the *Mauthe's* pilothouse, as the boat glides up the river, is Deck-Cadet Richard Ruth from the Great Lakes Maritime Academy. As part of their training, the cadets must sail 350 days, using multiple vessels of various fleets. Today, Richard has a neatly detailed and intricately hand-drawn chart of the Detroit and St. Clair rivers spread out in the chart room. His job is the seemingly impossible task of learning the rivers, while being taught and quizzed by the pilothouse crew. All around the boat, the cadet will repeat the process with all of the crew. For Richard, the *Mauthe* is a floating, hands-on classroom, open around the clock.

The Ambassador Bridge looms ahead, as the mail-boat *J.W. Westcott II* angles out to the *Mauthe*. The little boat is a lifeline providing much more than mail, since the freighters it serves never have to stop. Today the delivery consists of mail for the crew, some company items, a stack of Sunday papers and one special package, a centerpiece arrangement of flowers from "the flower lady." There are numerous stories as to why the flower lady sends arrangements to various boats as they pass, but the fact remains that Arlene Earl sends the arrangements and expects only a whistle salute in return. Passing Harsens Island, the master seizes the whistle-pull and sounds one long and two shorts, steps out onto the bridge-wing and gives a grateful wave as they pass the flower lady's house.

Darkness has fallen as the *Mauthe* approaches Stag Island and the captain checks the speed to a snail's crawl. Currently the *Callaway* is squatting at the Shell Oil fuel dock, just above the island and the *Mauthe* must hold back for the tin-stacker to clear. Shortly the *Callaway* calls the Interlake boat and advises that about 10 more minutes will be needed, as promised, the dock is clear in a half hour and the *Mauthe* eases up and makes her lines secure. A giant hose is put over the side and the dock proceeds to pump aboard 72,197 gallons of bunker-C diesel oil. The tanks can handle 149,000 gallons, but at an average consumption of 11,500 gallons per day, a substantial portion of what she is now taking aboard will be burned before she reaches the grain dock at Superior. In just over an hour the hose is back aboard and the steamer is headed through what remains of the St. Clair River and on to Lake Huron, as the 730-foot *Algosound* takes her place at the dock.

As hazardous as it is, late-season navigation does eliminate one menace from the lake mariner's job, for which they are eternally grateful and that is the careless pleasure boater. During pleasant weather the Detroit and St. Clair rivers are swarming with pleasure craft, most going about their leisure with careful consideration, but there are a few seeming to want a bit more. Unfortunately this often involves an elaborate game of dodging across the path of an oncoming lake freighter. With no consideration for the inability of a laker to stop suddenly or turn with any kind of urgency, these weekend sailors will turn their egg-shell frail fiberglass boats and cut directly in front of a passing steel monster lakeboat. The laker crew can only hold their collective breath, to see if the pleasure boat that disappeared from view comes again into sight. A big laker could easily crush a pleasure boat and the freighter's crew would never feel the impact. Most of the time the careless boaters emerge, shouting and laughing as if they have won some game. On board the *Mauthe* they tell the tale of another laker from which a pleasure craft did not reappear. When the oreboat crew dashed to the rail expecting to find people in the water, they found the pleasure craft up along side, with its occupants spray-painting graffiti on the freighter's beam! Clearly such incidents are rare and not all pleasure boaters are reckless, but there are enough to make the lakeboat crew appreciate the onset of foul weather, especially where the St. Clair River meets Lake Huron.

Into the blackness of Lake Huron the *Mauthe* churns. It is after midnight and a noticeable quiet fills the boat. Of course there is unending vigilance in the pilothouse and a constant watch in the engine room, but the crew not on duty are taking advantage of a rare commodity, the privacy of their rooms. Those on duty are performing the tedious painting and stowing tasks, common to a freighter, in various locations around the boat. Walking around the boat at this time of night, one could get the impression of being on some ghost ship. In the windlass room every item is in its place and only the sound of the waves pounding the bow breaks the stillness. A deck below, the washer and dryer and the crew's exercise equipment await use. On board boats of the *Mauthe's* class, one can pass from bow to stern by one of two tunnels, running along the boat's beam just below the spar deck. The tunnel is empty, too, and filled only by the loud noise of large fans, circulating overheated air. Astern, the scene is much the same as forward, except for more noise and vibration.

Galley accommodations on the *Mauthe* are in the stern and in the wee hours of the night, they too are vacant. Hanging pots and pans clang together and dinner left-overs are kept warm in big foil covered pans. Crew members who feel like a late night snack can help themselves or explore the big refrigerator for sandwich material. Three meals each day are served aboard the *Mauthe*, with the second cook serving the officer's dining room, the porter serving the crew's eating area and the cook reigning over the whole domain. Oddly, the galley is the one place on a lakeboat where the most formality can be sensed. On the *Mauthe*, seats are assigned at the officer's table by the second cook and plates are carefully set down in front of you, no need to reach up. The daily menu is listed on an erasable board and every meal is "all you can eat." The *Mauthe's* cook and galley czar Don Cook sees to that.

Meals on board the *Mauthe* are served on a schedule the crew know by heart. Supper is served from half past four o'clock in the afternoon until half past five and includes two kinds of meat and enough vegetables and trimmings to stuff the hungriest crewman. Lunch is a combination of breakfast items for crew whose duties will not allow them to make that meal, and mid-day sandwiches, burgers and salads, all served in the hour before noon. From 7:30 a.m. until 8:30 a.m. breakfast is presented and offers every selection and combination imaginable, including the finest blueberry pancakes on the planet. Crew members never really crowd the galley, they simply drift in at their convenience and leave well-fed. Meals are the opportunity for the crew to exchange the latest gossip, too, keeping with the tradition of the galley as the universal exchange point for unofficial ship's news.

Beating her way northward the *Mauthe* begins to face a continually stiffening wind. As the boat comes abeam Point aux Barques on the tip of Michigan's thumb, the winds are gusting to 40 miles-per-hour and gale warnings are up for Lake Huron. Meeting the eight to 12-foot seas nearly head-on, the big steamer is beginning to take spray over the rail. Her bluff bow pounds from time to time making a low "boom" sound, like the slamming of a distant warehouse door, the lake mariners say she's "stubbin' her toe." Spray is no problem, but the one thing the captain does not like to do is roll the boat and once the *Mauthe* clears the thumb, the west wind will put seas on her beam and she will roll. Just above the point, the boat is hauled around to the west and runs across the mouth of Saginaw Bay. To take advantage of the lee of land, the *Mauthe* is tucked up against the Michigan shore once more.

At dawn the winds are still blowing strong, at times strengthening to 40 miles-per-hour and lingering there. Still hugging the Michigan shore, the *Mauthe* is coming upon Alpena. A streak of black smoke comes from the shoreline and the *S.T. Crapo*, one of the last coal-burners, comes into binocular range. She is downbound for Alpena and hugging even closer to the coast. A single wave slaps the *Mauthe's* bow and throws a drenching spray onto the pilothouse windows, where it promptly freezes. This is December navigation.

Late afternoon on December 7th finds the snow whitened gap of Detour Passage greeting the big Interlake steamer. As forecast, the winds have faded to a gusty bluster and from the *Mauthe's* pilothouse the Coast Guard buoy tender *Buckthorn* is seen, lifting buoys from the Saint Marys River before the winter ice can crush them. Down in the *Mauthe's* windlass room the anchors are being "cleared." This work is performed before the boat goes into any river and involves removal of the equipment that prevents anchors from accidentally dropping. First the "devil's claws," two steel hooks supported by cables, are removed. These flat steel catches are hooked through a link in each of the anchor chains and should the equipment holding the chain slip, they are designed to keep the anchors aboard. Next, the wing-nuts holding down the steel plates covering the hawse pipes are removed and the plates lifted. The hawse pipe is the opening through which the anchor chain passes when let go and, although the *Mauthe's* are nearly a dozen feet long, the lake will often shoot up them in a rough sea. Supposedly, the covers are to keep the intruding water out, but such is not the case. Old pillows are stuffed beneath the plates aboard the *Mauthe* to block the lake and are, in fact, quite effective. When upbound, only the forward anchors need to be cleared, but downbound the stern anchor is also cleared. With her hooks free, the *Mauthe* pushes toward the Soo.

Like a sleeping Christmas display, the city of Sault Saint Marie slides past the *Mauthe* and with surgical care the crew lines the boat up, easing her toward the MacArthur lock. As the bow comes "up against," a crewman is swung over the side on the boom and the moment it can be swung back, a second crewman is sent over. Lines from the boat are passed to hands on the pier and the *Mauthe* moves into the lock. The whole scene resembles a cross between a long-running Broadway play and some sort of circus act. It is fascinating to spectators, but those who are performing have done it so many times, they barely give their work a second thought. With the chadburn ringing and the radio squawking, the *Mauthe* eases into the confines of the lock and the lower gates close behind. In less than an hour the process is complete and the steamer is headed toward open Lake Superior once more.

Steadily widening, the Saint Marys River opens into Whitefish Bay and, with the Lake Superior's temper well in mind, the captain retires for the night. The winds on this largest lake are out of the west and again reaching 40 miles-per-hour, but the waves are forming only a large dead swell. "If that wind shifts north come down and get me." The master's orders are unusually dour in tone: "I mean if it even starts swingin' anywhere near toward the north. I don't want it comin' at us like that while it's in the fourth notch." Lake Superior is never to be trifled with and a more northerly wind could set the *Mauthe* rolling in a beam sea. The "fourth notch" is slang that refers to the mayfor code attached to the wind velocity in knots with 0 being 0-10, 1 being 11-16, 2 being 17-21, 3 being 22-27, 4 being 28-33, 5 being 34-40, 6 being 41-47, 7 being 48-55, 8 being 56-63 and 9 being over 63. Late-season navigation demands constant vigilance, for a slight shift in the winds can lead to a howling gale.

Awaking with the first light of December 8th, the crew on the *Mauthe* can feel the deck barely moving beneath their feet. It would seem the boat is in shelter, but a quick glance from the port hole shows the steamer underway and making good time. The forecast gale has disintegrated and the boat is in the middle of the pleasant side of late-season sailing. Under calm sky and on top a nearly flat sea, the steamer churns through the day toward the head of the lakes.

At 90 turns of her giant propeller, the immense steamer produces 7000 horsepower and can make upwards of 15 miles-per-hour. The steam turbine engine, that pulses like a heart deep in her stern, sports a complex array of hissing pipes and gauges that distracts from the simplicity of the engine's basic operation. Water is drawn from the lake at a spot two miles above Whitefish Point or if running lower lakes routes, above Lake Michigan's Bone Reef, where the best is found and purified through condensers. The immaculate water is fed to the boilers and turned into steam. (It is interesting that the potable water used for drinking and cooking is taken at the same spots and used without purification, while the boiler's water must be far cleaner than the human's water.) Steam is next passed over a turbine and through the use of reduction gearing they turn the screw. Although the nuts and bolts of every system is complex, the basic function is this simple. All of this in no way makes Chief Liimatta and his staff's job a simple matter. They not only keep the original equipment of the *Mauthe's* engine workings moving smoothly, but they are responsible for everything else on the boat, from a leaky sink to a stubborn winch.

Three miles away from the Duluth canal, the *Mauthe* radios the famous aerial lift bridge that spans the waterway. The bridge tender has had the lights of the Interlake boat in sight for a long while and the radio call is just a formality. What is not a formality is the conversation between the *Mauthe* and Algoma Marine's 730-foot motor vessel *Algowest*, loading at the Harvest States number 1 dock, the *Mauthe's* destination. Five more minutes and the *Algowest* will vacate that dock and head over to the Cargill B1 dock for the rest of her Seaway bound cargo. What is advantageous to the *Mauthe* is that ice, three inches thick in some places, has formed within the harbor and the *Algowest* will break up most of it, before the Interlake boat gets there.

Passing gingerly through the cement piers of the ship canal, the *Mauthe* encounters only thin, floating ice. The crunch of the ice is not heard from the bow, until the boat approaches Rices Point, where the pack is well broken up by the *Algowest*. Around the turn at West Gate Basin, the water is open and the steamer angles in toward the dock with ease. By half past ten the *Mauthe's* beam is being made fast to the Harvest States dock, but the loading shoots and crews will not work until morning. The empty steamer will wait through the night.

For more than 13 hours, grain shoots down the spouts into the Interlake boat's yawning holds. Compartments 2, 3 and 4 will receive a combined total of 480,000 bushels of Protein 14.3 at 60.4 pounds per bushel, while compartment number 1 will be filled with 141,000 bushels of Protein 15.3 at 60.5 pounds per bushel. This entire burden will give the boat a loaded draft of 22.5-feet forward, 23.1 midships and 23.8 aft. All of this raises the question "what is Protein 14.3 and 15.3, where does it come from, and what will it be used for?" If asked, the loading workers ashore and especially the crew of the *Mauthe* will answer that the point is moot. It does not matter what it is, or where it comes from or even what it is to be used for, it is just grain taken at the head of the lakes that needs to be hauled to Buffalo. After this cargo they will haul another and perhaps a couple of others, and soon the long 1992 season will be over and they will go home to their families. After a more than 14 million bushel season, it most assuredly is "just grain."

At 11:33 p.m. Duluth time, December 10th, 1992, the Interlake steamer *J.L. Mauthe* slips again beneath the aerial lift bridge and soon is well onto open Lake Superior. Noting her departure time, the wheelsmen each privately calculate the boat's estimated time at the Soo Locks, the St. Clair and Detroit rivers and Buffalo breakwater, in an attempt to guess who will get the tough wheelin'. The Chief figures his fuel versus cargo, to get a good number for the fuel load to be taken on the next upbound stop at the Shell dock. In his room, the deck cadet works on another of the multiple projects he must complete and down the passageway the galley staff is sound asleep in anticipation of their normal early morning start. From the pilothouse window the captain looks out across the lake and thinks about the Ohio Street turn. All around the boat, the

Downbound at the Soo the J.L. Mauthe *is seen in her last years as a steamer. D.J. Story Photo*

crew is wondering how many more trips will there be this season, as the light-studded hills of Duluth-Superior fade astern.

Sunrise illuminates the boat's crew as they busy themselves hosing off the grain and dust accumulated in every corner of the vessel. Wet grain is shoveled over the side and the rest runs from the scuppers. The fish along the downbound routes from the upper lakes grain ports must be the best nourished in the world. Thus the routine of the *Mauthe* goes on all the way down to Buffalo, the only thing breaking the monotony, the emergency drill. This trip it is a fire drill, the crew don lifejackets and survival suits and squirt the fire hoses over the side fore and aft, to simulate fighting a fire. Rumor has it that on hot summer days, to break the heat, the aft crew pretends that the forward crew is afire and vice versa, thus hosing down one another.

At long last, in the wee hours of Sunday morning, the *Mauthe* is once again at the Standard Elevator, her crew preparing to start the whole routine again. To them, this whole business is not romantic or adventurous, it is just grain. It is their job, simply, Trip 29.

The season of 1992 was one of the last that the *Mauthe* would see as a self propelled steamer. She ran a few trips in 1993, but was laid up for the final time on July 5th, 1993 in Superior, Wisconsin. She remained in lay-up there until the last day of December 1996 when she was towed downbound to Sturgeon Bay for conversion to a self-unloading barge. It is an abominable trend on the lakes that has led many a classic lakeboat to be neutered and returned to service attached to the bow of a tug.

There are several business advantages to these mutilations where a classic lake freighter is cut down into a barge that makes the process more highly palatable to the shipping companies. The first is cost, both in the way of staffing and general operations. Since barges suffer from far fewer Coast Guard regulations than to powered vessels, removing the engine from a ounce proud lakeboat and calling it a barge allows the craft to operate without a crew. The crew that does tend to the barge can be housed on

At the wall in Duluth in August 1994 the once proud steamer J.L. Mauthe *awaits her fate. Author's Photo*

whatever tug happens to be pushing or pulling the barge. That crew can consist of less than half of the number of mariners that once staffed the same hull when it was a powered boat. This means that the operating cost is also cut in half. A barge is also not subject to the Coast Guard's five year hull inspections and so it can run, literally, until its bottom falls out. Additionally, when the cargo rates are low, the barge can simply be laid-up with almost no maintenance expense and wait until the cargo market improves. Also, in winter conditions, while the barge is unloading, the tug can release and then move around the area breaking ice and keeping the barge free for its departure.

Arguably, critics of these huge tug-barge conversions say that there is one big downside to the practice, safety. Although the new tugs that shove these barges are equipped with the very latest in navigation equipment, all of that technology can easily be hauled to the bottom of the lake by a foundering barge. There is a good reason why hull inspections of powered vessels are required and it is not just because the vessel has an engine. The elongated hull of any vessel in rough weather suffers the greatest strain and stress. If the hull of a barge goes forever uninspected the day is going to come when it is no longer seaworthy. Additionally, the human factor of no inspection being required equating to continuing to run the boat until it can physically run no more comes into play. This all leads to a dangerous situation where economy leads to disaster.

Through the year of 1997 the torches cut away at the *Mauthe's* hull at the Bay Shipbuilding Company, Sturgeon Bay, Wisconsin. Her cabins were removed and her engine compartment gutted. A large "V" notch was added to her stern and fitted with securing accommodations for her tug. Soon her name was painted out on her bow and the hull was refloated from the dry-dock in late November. Next, unlike other self-unloaders which have hopper shaped holds her hold was replaced with a flat bottom cargo hold and a tunnel belt and loop belt system capable of discharging a wide variety of cargoes. This flat bottom hold allows for greater cargo capacity, but prevents the cargoes from dropping by gravity through the trap doors onto the

Transformed into a barge the former J.L. Mauthe now serves as the Pathfinder. D.J. Story Photo

The former J.L. Mauthe, *now in service as the barge*
Pathfinder. *D.J. Story Photo*

unloading belt. For that reason front-end loaders were
built into the hold and are used to manually shove the
cargo into the unloading traps. A 260' unloading boom
was added to her deck to facilitate unloading. After the
13-million dollar rebuild, the barge was renamed
Pathfinder and took her first cargo in Escanaba,
Michigan, on March 20, 1998.

Although a special tug was planned for the
Pathfinder, the tug's construction was not started until
the first day of January, 1998 and it would be nine
months before it was ready to join the former *Mauthe*.
Until then the barge would be pushed by the tug *Joyce
L. Van Enkevort*. On September 15, 1998 the new 124-
foot, 7,200 horsepower tug *Dorothy Ann* was taken

charge of by the Interlake Steamship Company. Using what is called an articulated pin-type connection system the *Dorothy Ann* was connected to the *Pathfinder's* notched stern. Two hydraulic rams projecting from the sides of the tug's bow were locked into receptacles in the barge's stern and the combination of tug and barge made their first combined trip on June 26, 1989. With that, the *J.L. Mauthe* became nothing more than a memory.

BELLES AND THIEVES

Author's note: This story was originally published in my 1993 book "Ice Water Museum." Since that time, significant discoveries have been made concerning the events contained in the text. For that reason this corrected and up-dated version of the text is published here. If you have read this story before, trust me... you will want to read it again!

On the second day of September, 1879, the summer seemed to be unwilling to let go of the Great Lakes. A protracted drought had gripped the region and repeated heat waves had swept the area. In the communities of East Saginaw and West Saginaw, the streets steamed with a mixture of hay and hot manure from the assorted animals used in everyday life while the wooden sidewalks seemed to moan with each step taken upon them. Early that morning, all around the town, windows were propped open to let the heat out, even though they also let the bugs in. Window screens, although in existence in 1879, could cost a home owner as much as six dollars per window. For most folks, that was nearly a week's wages or more, so most homes were without screens. Also it was a widely held myth in that era that the thick night air held suspended many of the things that caused common disease and it was best to close your home up tightly during the night and not let the summer air in. It was thought best to wait until the morning heat had burned off the damp air before opening your windows. So people commonly sweltered in otherwise cool summer nights, only to open their windows to greet the heat of the day. Kids swam in the Saginaw River to beat the heat. It was an activity that would be unthinkable a century later due to pollution by toxic chemicals. Other kids simply looked for shade as they awaited the beginning of the school year. The *Saginaw Morning Herald* newspaper was prompted to comment that due to the heat, "There was a notable scarcity of cows and children in the streets yesterday," a condition of which half still exists today.

Moored at Stewart's lumber dock, the steamer *Jacob Bertschy* also had all of her cabin windows propped open, even though there was no breeze to be found. In the stuffy stillness of his cabin Captain G. W. McGregor lay in his bed as sick as a dog. Although history leaves us no record as to his exact illness, it is on record that he was incapacitated to the point where he was simply forced to stay in his cabin. Thus, the boat was in the charge of First Mate John L. McIntosh during the captain's illness. Second Mate H. Roach was doubling

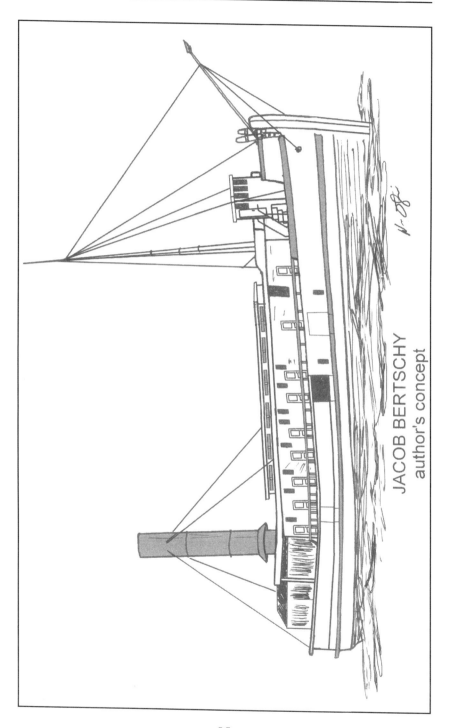

JACOB BERTSCHY
author's concept

as ship's clerk because Charles McIntosh, the assigned ship's clerk, had been forced to remain at his home in Detroit when the *Bertschy* headed out to Saginaw. He too was listed as being incapacitated with an "illness." There is, again, no record to tell us if he and the captain were both suffering from similar illnesses. But what is on the records is that the ship's clerk, Charles McIntosh, was also the owner of the *Bertschy*; the boat was in every way a McIntosh family business.

Coming across the gangways and being loaded into the belly of the *Bertschy* was a load of just over 1.2 million wooden shingles. Although this sounds like a massive cargo, it was actually only a portion of what she could carry. She would eventually stop at Tawas and load another 200,000 shingles. Ownership of her cargo divides into a small who's-who of lumber barons of the era. Rust, King & Clint were the firm that owned the largest portion of the load with a stake in 400,000 shingles, E.P. Sheldon owned 200,000 shingles, A.T. Bliss owned 240,000 of the shingles, James Steward owned 117,500 shingles and 250,000 were listed in the ownership of "C & E Ten Eyck." Most of these names would go on to cultivate empires in the lumber business over the next decade, but all would one day vanish with the decline of the lumber industry. Although this many shingles may sound like a huge amount, for the lumber giants who had ownership of the cargo, it was simply another day's load.

Shingles, however, were not the only things coming aboard the *Bertschy* on that hot dry Wednesday morning. Her trip was also scheduled to stop at Port Austin where she would take on 318 bushels of wheat from Neill and Son as well as 25 bags of wheat from Cooper & Company. Saginaw merchant G. T. Zaschoerner had loaded aboard a large amount of household goods that he was shipping down to J. Jenks & Company of Sand Beach. Also coming aboard were 17 passengers and their belongings. There was a Mr. Reed, of Cleveland, and his daughter who arrived and strode up the wooden gangplank. Traveling companions listed as Miss Johnston and Miss Harvey were both headed for Detroit along with passengers J. Kelley, H.Y. Candon and T. Stickle, while John Miller and John Potter were headed for Goderich by way of Detroit. James Montgomery and his wife were headed for Sand Beach on Michigan's thumb while Mrs. Foote was headed for Grindstone City on the very tip of the thumb. The rest of the passengers, Miss Richards and Miss Locke, both of Bay City, have no destination listed.

Most out of place among the passengers were two true southern belles. They were the sisters of South Saginaw resident John Buckley and their names are lost to us as of this writing. Instead history identifies them simply as Misses "K.J." and "A." Buckley. What we do know about them is that they had come north to Saginaw to escape yellow fever that was sweeping across Memphis in this era. A mild winter, extended spring and scorching summer in 1878 made conditions right for another outbreak of Yellow Fever. Remembering that in 1873 more than 2,000 residents of Memphis had died of Yellow Fever, the Buckley sisters fled the city, along with about 25,000 other residents. The ladies had to go north, because fleeing Memphis residents were encountering quarantines throughout the south. While the Buckley sisters spent the next year in Saginaw, the fever killed 5,150 of their neighbors. Now, word was that the cold winter had brought relief from the fever to Memphis and the sisters thought it was safe to venture back to what they considered to be a more civilized way of life. Thus they had packed their entire wardrobe of fine southern dresses, shoes and garnishes in a number of massive trunks. The trunks were lugged aboard the *Bertschy* as the sisters politely walked aboard the vessel, fans in hand, gently waving just above the nose.

As far as water transportation down the lakes, the Buckley belles could hardly have chosen a better vessel to book passage upon. Although she had been constructed in 1867 at Sheboygan, Wisconsin, the original work of shipbuilder A.C. Stokes had been nearly obliterated in a fire in 1872, so her passenger cabins were newer than her keel. Remodeling and repair of the boat cost a then staggering $10,000. Work advanced rapidly, however, and the boat, with her new upper works went back to work just in time to run aground in a storm off of Escanaba, Michigan that November. She may not have been the luckiest boat on the lakes, but she had some of the most elegant accommodations of any lakeboat of her class. She is, in fact, one of the very few boats ever to run out of the

Saginaw River that actually has listed as members of her crew, two "musicians," French Morgan and William Fish. From 1876 to 1879 the *Bertschy* doubled as an excursion boat, taking passengers on tours of Lake Huron and Lake Erie and was quite popular with the upper class of Saginaw and Bay City residents.

Officially, the *Bertschy* measured in at 138-feet long, 434 tons. She was of propeller build in an era when side wheelers were still popular. Her hull was made of oak planking and her engine was powered by steam. For the most part, that's about all that we know for certain about the boat. No known photos or drawings exist of her and her lifespan was quite short. In looking at similar vessels of her class we can say that she likely had side ports through which cargo of any sort could be loaded. Small combination passenger and cargo vessels such as the *Bertschy* were very common around the great lakes in the mid 1800s. They made their living, as she did, hopping from one small port to another and transporting passengers from lakeside towns to the big cities of the lower lakes such as Detroit and Cleveland.

All through the heat of Wednesday morning the dock wallopers worked at loading the cargo aboard the while her crew went about their chores. The ship's porters, George Waters and Hiram Bennett went about seeing to the needs of the passengers, first getting the guests into their assigned staterooms, then seeing if they needed anything. As the morning wore on and the guests began to wander about the deck, the ship's waiters, Walton and McIntosh, were always present to offer what refreshment could be presented. Shortly before departure time, as the passengers gathered in the boat's grand parlor, a single throaty blast from the boat's whistle startled most of them. It was the signal that the *Bertschy*, her lines now cast off, was leaving the dock. Many of the passengers who had kinfolk ashore stepped out to the boat's thick wooden rail to wave goodbye. Others simply wanted to watch the scenery and bridges pass and a few remained in the parlor, sipping cold drinks and wishing for any hint of a breeze that the boat's motion may bring. In the cramped galley Chief Cook William Thomas was hard at work preparing the lunch as his assistant cook prepared the appetizers. Although the second cook's name is recorded only as H. Perry we can imagine that his efforts in passenger comfort and satisfaction were just as high as the rest of the boat's crew and he was indeed whipping up something tasty and refreshing.

Through the afternoon the *Bertschy* slid silently along the Saginaw River. Her passengers watched in amazement as the bustle of steam tugs, schooners, barges, steamers and rafts seemed to swarm along the river. Whistles hooted and smokestacks huffed as sometimes the *Bertschy* seemed to miss striking something by just a few inches. Of course Wheelsman Holliday knew the river in his sleep and First Mate John McIntosh could almost predict every movement of every floating object so the *Bertschy* simply sailed along without a snag. Ashore the sawmills hummed as millions of board feet of timber was being cut. It seemed as if every square foot of riverbank was occupied by a mill of some sort. Likewise, a half dozen swing bridges needed to be threaded by the steamer. The river itself was actually a two lane highway and often as one vessel passed through one side of an open bridge, another passed going through the adjoining draw in the opposite direction. No sooner had the *Bertschy* cleared the last bridge in Saginaw than she came upon the elbow turn at the village of Carrollton and the dreaded "Carrollton Bar." This was an area just north of the village where the river's flow tended to build up silt and always caused passing vessels a good deal of trouble. From there it was a brief zigzag to get past Crow Island abeam of the town of Zilwaukee. After Crow Island the scenery turned into a near wilderness for the next five miles with the steady march of traffic on the river being the only clue to the level of human activity. In an almost constant series of hoots, the *Bertschy's* whistle sounded passing signals as vessels of every sort passed. There were tugs hauling schooners and schooner-barges, and massive rafts of logs. There were steamers with lumber and steamers with passengers all hustling to get the most out of their day's work. Then just over an hour from Crow Island, McGraw's dock and the city of Portsmouth simply popped into view. This was the south end of the shipping center of Bay City. If Saginaw was the foundation of the monarchy of king lumber, Bay City was its Camelot. The river traffic and activity increased three fold as the *Bertschy* came abeam of Stone's

Island and pointed her bow toward the swing of the 23rd Street Bridge. Stone's Island, known in modern times simply as "The Middle Grounds" sported a saw mill and three docks and along the entire waterfront of Bay City there were an additional 30 mills. Likewise salt works garnished the shore as did shipyards and docks. It was the sort of scenery that drew most of the *Bertschy's* passengers out to the rail to watch it all pass.

There is no clear record as to whether the *Bertschy* stopped in Bay City or not. She did, however, have aboard one passenger from Bay City, listed as "Miss Locke" and in his statement to reporters several days later Captain McGregor says that the *Bertschy* "...left Bay City at 3 o'clock Wednesday afternoon..." Thus all we can say for certain is that around dinner time, the *Bertschy* was pointing her steering pole toward the expanse of Saginaw Bay. By this time, the hot and hazy conditions of Wednesday morning had taken on a drastic change. The wind had come up into a stiff blow from the east and the formerly calm surface of the bay had turned into a choppy mess. Almost as soon as the *Bertschy* cleared the mouth of the river, she took on a bit of a roll as the seas were aided by the wind in trying to toss her about. Her acting captain set course for Tawas and ordered her ahead at full steam. The course was so well known to John McIntosh that he could have run it in his sleep and no charts were needed. He simply ran her north, nor' east until he caught sight of the Charity Island lighthouse. After passing the light he steered the *Bertschy* to put the lighthouse on his southeast and ran north until he caught sight of the lighthouse on Ottawa Point, which is today called Tawas Point. From there the Tawas City dock was in sight as were the mill docks. Just as darkness began to set in, McIntosh was maneuvering the *Bertschy* firmly to the dock where she would receive her additional cargo of shingles. It was also about that time that the rain began to fall.

At first the passengers, who were settling in one by one for the night, hardly noticed the rain. Rather it was the fresh breeze that came across the lake which gained everyone's attention. Soon, however, the hiss of sheets of rain on the *Bertschy's* decks and the moan of wind in her rigging told of summer's end and autumn's arrival. The waves came directly in off of the lake and marched right along the dock with no break. The Tawas dock was unsheltered from a due east wind and this one was building waves all the way from the Canadian shore. McIntosh ordered extra line out and the boat simply sat there and rubbed herself against the pier as if she were itching to get the trip going once more.

Thursday morning brought no relief from the weather for the *Bertschy* and her people. In the dining hall the kitchen and serving staff had served an early breakfast. It was their way of saying that the trip down the lake was going to be a rough one. By 10 o'clock that morning the boat was nearly a quarter million shingles heavier and was headed out onto open Lake Huron. The wind was still out of the east and blowing hard, but the *Bertschy* was headed to the seas and making good weather of it, especially when compared to the rolling she had done the day before.

In her pilothouse it was nearly impossible to see more than a boat-length or two ahead as the driving rain obscured the glass. Opening a window was not an option because of the heavy rain and heavy spray coming over the bow. There were only the waves coming from out of the gray distance to be seen. If another vessel were to come across the *Bertschy's* path, her pilothouse crew would have no time to react. Still acting as captain, First Mate McIntosh simply slogged the boat ahead on a compass heading of 120-degrees. If he held his course and the winds did not shift the *Bertschy* should have Port Austin off her steering pole a bit after three o'clock in the afternoon. It was shaping up to be a long, wet and rough afternoon.

Down in the galley, Chief Cook Thomas was preparing the afternoon meal as if there was no weather at all to deal with. He was determined that his staff would not let the boat's passengers suffer inconvenience by a touch of weather. Of course the major part of the suffering on this afternoon was not from the lack of food, but rather from trying to keep it down. A trip to the *Bertschy's* rail to relieve one's seasickness and feed Lake Huron's fish would be unpleasant in more ways than one. With gale force winds blowing, rain pelting and spray unexpectedly boarding, anyone not in tune with their sea legs would be better to stay in their room and remain clear of food until the trip was over.

As the rain developed into a series of squalls and acting captain McIntosh spied the Port Austin shore in the distance, and took his bearings on the tall smokestack of the Ayres sawmill. Making the dock was no problem since the lee of Michigan's thumb would block the wind and seas. Port Austin was the last bit of good shelter from an easterly gale before making the long downbound haul to Port Huron. Once at the dock the crew went to work loading the barrels and bags of wheat. Just as the last of the cargo came aboard, however, the wind began to shift and waves came rolling from as far north as the Straits of Mackinaw. Now the *Bertschy* began to pound at the dock and worse yet, began to pound her hull on the bottom. To McIntosh it was clear that Port Austin was no longer a shelter and he needed to get the *Bertschy* under way. Still, McIntosh consulted with Captain McGregor who, from his sickbed, agreed with the action. What neither man knew was that Lake Huron had just lured them into a classic trap from which there was no escape. Indeed the only option on this voyage that would have spared the *Bertschy* would have been to keep her tied to the dock at Tawas and, from everyone's perspective, there was no reason to have done that.

Just as the kitchen staff was serving dinner to the passengers and the two southern belles were beginning to exercise their best table manners, the sound of the wind in the boat's wires took on a new and frightening howl. The dinner table seemed to move as the entire vessel lurched and rolled in an awful manner. Plates slid and cups teetered as everyone, guests and serving staff alike, reached out instinctively to capture the sliding dinnerware. A moment later the entire scene tilted in the other direction as the *Bertschy's* oak hull gave out a deep groan.

Up in the pilothouse John McIntosh held on as his mind raced to make the next decision. He immediately shouted down the speaking tube and ordered the engine ahead full. With the winds blowing out of the north, and their intensity had grown substantially, it was now McIntosh and the *Bertschy* against Lake Huron. This direction of wind found the *Bertschy* fully exposed to waves. McIntosh knew full well that the waves, now being 8- to 15-feet high, would expose the actual lake bottom in the shallow areas around where he currently had the *Bertschy*. Before he could get the boat fully away from the dock she took a series of large waves. With a few bone jarring thuds she solidly struck her bottom. Now she would pound herself to pieces in minutes if this happened again. All McIntosh could do was to run for deeper water.

In his cabin Captain McGregor was struggling to get his trousers on as his boat continued to lurch beneath him. By the time he got to the pilothouse, McIntosh already had her moving well out into the lake. She was on a slightly northwest course to avoid the Port Austin Reef and her crew would run her up until the mill's smokestack looked to be in the right position to allow them to turn and clear the reef. Although the recently established Port Austin reef lighthouse was in working order, McIntosh, like most mariners, trusted his own judgment more than the survey's of the US Government. When Captain McGregor took command once again, he simply kept to McIntosh's course. He knew, like his first mate, that their only choice now was to run the *Bertschy* into deep water and try and stay clear of the shoreline and its teeth of boulders. The entire lake bottom along the tip of Michigan's thumb is a series of shallow shelves and reefs extending as far as two miles from shore that are all peppered with ice-age boulders. Soon Lake Huron would have the *Bertschy* caught between that and its huge waves with the boat having no choice other than to keep running.

There is nothing that a captain likes to do less than roll the boat. Rolling in the seas can cause cargo to break loose, equipment to be damaged and people to be hurt. Worse yet, a rolling hull tends to bend and twist which causes hull components to open up and the seas to flood in. Some classes of vessels, such as modern steel hulled boats can stand up to a great deal of severe rolling. Wooden hulled steamers, such as the *Bertschy*, could tolerate very little severe rolling. Now, Captain McGregor and Mate McIntosh had no choice other than to run her and hope she would be able to take the punishment.

After clearing the reef, just after seven o'clock that evening, Captain McGregor ordered the *Bertschy* onto a nearly due east heading. He called down to the engine room and ordered her to be given all she had. Now the pilothouse crew watched as the waves out of the north predictably grew. She rolled, she twisted, she groaned and soon, she began to leak. Chief Engineer John Morgan started the boat's steam pumps in an effort to stop the flooding. For a time it seemed to work, but within an hour the pumps became choked and simply stopped working. After reporting this event to the pilothouse, Chief Morgan and his second, Dan McMullen, immediately went to work on repairing the pumps. The *Bertschy* was now just rounding the Thumb and was just above Grindstone City when the word came that the pumps were out. For a while Captain McGregor had considered running back to Port Austin, but the pumps had made the decision for him. Port Austin may as well have been on another lake at this point. There was not enough time to turn the *Bertschy* and run there. He decided to turn and run into Grindstone City.

Grindstone City, although established as a community in the 1830s, was not given its official name until 1876. The town consisted of a large quarry where raw grindstone material was mined, a salt well and two earthen piers that each extended just over 1,000-feet into the lake. It was Captain McGregor's intention to run the *Bertschy* up between those piers and allow her to settle in the shallow and protected water where her passengers could be easily off loaded. He got his boat turned, but no sooner had he finished the turn than a huge cloud of steam swallowed the stern of the boat. The lake had flooded in to the point where it had now reached the boat's firebox and snuffed it out. The chief had only one choice and that was to let off the steam pressure as fast as he could in order to prevent an explosion when the water reached the boiler itself. Now, the *Bertschy* was adrift and without power, just a few boat-lengths from safety.

Passengers aboard the *Bertschy* were not unaware of the boat's condition. They had all been informed that the boat was in a leaking condition and that they were headed for shore. When the engine became disabled and the vessel went adrift, the passengers found themselves looking over the boat's rail toward scenery of a different sort. Through the blackness of the night and a vale of driving rain only a very few dim amber lamps marked the shore. Dry land seemed so distant yet was just over 1,000-feet away. The situation was disorienting yet none of the passengers was driven to panic. Even when the low rumbling crunch of the *Bertschy's* oak bottom being driven solidly onto the boulders of the bottom was heard, no one panicked. The atmosphere of calm in the storm was seeded primarily by the cool heads of the boat's crew. They quickly went about working on a way to get help and to get safely ashore.

Immediately after the boat grounded, Captain McGregor ordered one of the lifeboats launched and in it were John McIntosh, Second Mate Roach and four other crewmen. At first the lifeboat appeared to get away cleanly, but no sooner had it cleared the lee of the *Bertschy's* hull than it was swamped and capsized by Lake Huron. All six occupants surfaced and clung to the overturned yawl as it was blown off into the darkness toward the rocky shore. Just before midnight, a second lifeboat was prepared. This time just one man was placed in the boat and a line was attached to it. Again, Lake Huron made short work of the attempt as it broke the line and set the boat and its lone passenger adrift down the shore and into the night. As far as anyone aboard the *Bertschy* knew at this point, they had already lost seven people to the angry lake. It was decided to wait for daylight before trying anything more. Now, all that the crew and passengers of the once proud *Bertschy* could do was to wait while the relentless waves crashed against her wooden hull and threatened to take her apart timber by timber. It seemed as if daylight had never been so far away as it was that night.

In reality, the seven souls washed away into that black night were not lost at all. In fact the first six had simply hung on to the lifeboat and drifted onto the rocks about a half mile down the beach. Although the wind and rain were cold, the water, by Lake Huron standards, was actually quite warm. With only a few scrapes and bruises the first six castaways found their way onto some high rocks and, for the time being, out of danger. They were beneath a bluff and with the rain and wind, the face of the bluff was too slippery to climb. So, like their shipmates aboard the stranded *Bertschy*, they were forced to simply wait for daylight. The only true danger now would be if the *Bertschy* herself began to break up. Then huge pieces of her would be driven ashore right where the castaways were stranded crushing the poor souls like bugs. In the distance they could see her lamps and McGregor told the boys to keep an eye out for pieces of the boat. A few hours later a piece of the steamer did come ashore, it was the second lifeboat and its lone castaway. He too had easily survived the lake only to wind up on the rocks with his fellow crewmen safe, but stranded.

Grudgingly, dawn began to arrive at Grindstone City as the winds and waves continued to pound at the stranded steamer. With the first hints of daylight the local citizens of the tiny town quickly discovered the shipwreck just off shore. Cool heads prevailed that morning as the best rider and fastest horse in town were sent to the Point aux Barques life-saving station to summon the storm warriors. Shortly after the rider had been dispatched, the local folks assembled a team of horses able to pull the life-savers wagons and sent it along behind the rider. The logic here was to speed the process, as the station's team of horses would surely tire and slow down along the way to the wreck. This second, fresh team would meet them along the way and take over the chore of pulling the rescue equipment. At seven o'clock on the morning of September 4, the swift rider reached the life-saving station whose crew sprang into action. The station keeper sent for a local team of horses that the station kept on alert. In just a few minutes the boat-wagon, surfboat and equipment were hitched up and on the move.

At the same time as the life-savers were being alerted, another rescue effort was beginning at

Grindstone City. This was the discovery and rescue of the seven stranded castaways who were squatting on the boulders of the local beach. From up on the bluff someone had spotted them and soon ropes were lowered and all seven crewmen bumped, bruised and scuffed their way from the rocks to dry land.

"Spirited" was the word used to describe the team of horses that had left the life-saving station hauling the boat-wagon. Although they had been engaged to do so in advance, this team had never actually had to pull this strange load before. The horses were young and gave every indication that they would break away and run wild at any moment taking the surfboat and all the equipment with them! Fortunately, good life-savers in this era were also, by nature, good horsemen. They kept the team together and by the second mile, the chore had taxed the "spirit" out of the animals. Shortly there after the life-savers met up with the relief team sent from Grindstone City. Instead of shifting his wagons, however, the station keeper decided to send the relief team and one of his surfmen back to the station to get the beach cart and Lyle gun. Then the now de-spirited team and the boat-wagon pressed on toward the wreck, another five miles up the road.

Meanwhile, aboard the *Bertschy*, the daylight had brought some relief and some dread. The shipwrecked people aboard had watched with great relief as the seven castaways were hauled one-by-one up the bluff to safety, then the *Bertschy's* people stood in dread as the hull of the steamer began to come apart in the surf.

The crew passed out lifebelts to the passengers as the boat began to moan and shudder. Soon huge pieces of her side began to break away. The lake came into her hold and began to plunder her cargo. Millions of wood shingles were carried away by Lake Huron's waves and then the trunks and boxes belonging to her passengers were washed, one-by-one, from the hold and sent ashore. As it turned out, the lake would not be the only one stealing from the wreck that day. As the first of the passenger's trunks washed ashore, scavengers appeared from out of the tree-line. Local thieves who normally resided in the deep woods had gotten wind of a shipwreck and came to the edge of the forest in hopes of plunder. Each time an item of passenger baggage would wash ashore they would run out, grab it and haul it to the tree-line. There they would break it open and rob it of its contents, then vanish back into the gloom of the deep forest until another goodie would wash up.

From the *Bertschy* the helpless passengers could only watch as time and again their possessions were stolen. The most valued trunks belonged to the Buckley belles. They stood at the rail and could do nothing more than watch as the scavengers robbed their trunks and reveled in a thieves delight at the contents, then vanished again into the woods. "Like hawks on a chicken," Captain McGregor sneered as he watched the disgusting show of thievery. Indeed, nearly every piece of the passengers possessions which had been stored in the *Bertschy's* hull was plundered, leaving the passengers with nothing more than the clothes on their backs.

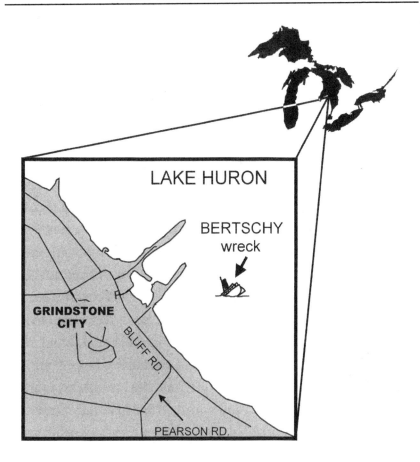

It was nine o'clock in the morning when the life-savers arrived at the wreck site. Immediately, they launched their surfboat. The rain was still coming down in sheets and the winds were still strong, but on the south pier more than 500 local residents watched the rescue effort begin. By now the starboard side of the boat was collapsed and she was heeled over into the seas. With the precision of a drill team the surfmen launched their boat and took to their oars. The sight of their surfboat slicing toward the wreck inspired some of the local men to attempt the same in a small fishing boat; they did not get far. In short order the lake sent the local men and their little boat fleeing back to the pier in a sinking condition. As the lifesavers reached the wreck a line was tossed from the *Bertschy* and grabbed by the storm warriors. Using it, two of the surfmen went into the water and then pulled themselves up and aboard the wreck. From the steamer's deck they would now direct the evacuation of the *Bertschy's* people.

Eleven ladies and one young boy were taken ashore by the life-savers in the first load. It was rough going but as they came ashore onto the earthen pier, the keeper told his crew of lifesavers that he was sure the vessel was going to pieces. "By the way that her stanchions are cracking and her cabins are settling, she cannot last long lads," he told them. They responded by making three more trips in the space of the next hour and plucking every person from the decks of the doomed *Bertschy*. Captain McGregor was the last person to go over the rail.

Just as the last load of survivors landed on the pier, the team of horses with the Lyle gun and beach cart arrived on the scene, just in time to be sent back to the station, in case another wreck should take place in the area. The lifesavers would stay at the wreck site for the next 24 hours, protecting what valuables remained. By dinner time the storm eased and the life-savers took their surfboat and made several trips out to the wreck bringing back what few passenger possessions that were left behind as well as cabin furniture and other goods. The steamer's crew went down the shore and found the area where the thieves had plundered the passenger's trunks, almost nothing but the empty and broken trunks remained. At six o'clock on Friday evening, the day following the rescue, the passengers and crew of the *Bertschy* departed Grindstone City on their way to Detroit aboard the steamer *Evening Star*. As the *Evening Star* snaked its way down the St. Clair River, Captain McGregor was still stewing over the sight of the thieves coming out of the woods and plundering the passenger's possessions. The insurance on the *Bertschy* would cover the losses of her passengers, but that was about all. He grumbled to Captain McRae of the *Evening Star* that the locals of Grindstone City knew who the thieves were and had said that they were people from nearby Huron City. "If our piano had drifted ashore, they'd have stolen that too."

SIGNED
PATRICK HOWE

It was a fair autumn day when Patrick Howe popped through the door of the John S. Parsons ship chandlery down on Water Street in Oswego, New York. Normally Parsons' establishment was a center of traffic for those who docked in the port as well as the local telegraph office, but Patrick was not there to send a wire. The ring of the bell above the door attracted the attention of merchant Parsons, who clopped forward across the worn hardwood floor. Much to his surprise, the storekeeper found not a customer, but his new friend Mr. Howe, standing at the counter with a large painting tucked under his arm.

As Mr. Parsons approached, Patrick held out the painting canvas for the merchant to admire. " It's fer you." the amateur artist said, "I painted it, it's the river here in Oswego." Mr. Parsons happily accepted the painting and promptly posted it where every customer could appreciate it. Parsons was a collector of amateur art and boat models that those who sailed the lakes were fond of producing, and this would be a welcome addition to his private collection.

Patrick Howe had not been long in the Oswego area and his current employment as cook on board the steamer *Homer Warren* kept him moving in and out of that port. Before that he had sailed the saltwater seas, but the jumble of the First World War had brought him to the lakes. Except for those aboard the boat, he had few friends in his newly-adopted home, but did make the acquaintance of merchant Parsons. Every time the *Warren* put her lines out at Oswego, Patrick made his way to Parsons to buy supplies for his galley and engage in some friendly conversation. This was the era when a friendly neighbor could stroll into a store and just stand about chatting with the owner. It was the autumn of 1919.

Hunched at the docks at Oswego, the 180-foot wooden lumber hooker *Homer Warren* had a belly full of corn. It was the 25th day of October and the boat's cargo was Toronto-bound under the supervision of Captain William Stocker, a resident of Toronto. Exactly why the *Warren* was about to depart Oswego with corn in her hold is a bit of a mystery. The reason why this is such a poser is that sending corn westward across the Great Lakes is sending it the wrong way on a one way street. Cargoes such as grain or corn normally travel from west to east across the freshwater seas. The reason for this is because the vast farmlands of the United States and Canada are located in the west while the great consumers of those products are located in the

Sporting the lines of a typical lumber hooker, the Homer Warren spent most of her career shuttling freight on the lower lakes.

east. Ports such as Buffalo, Montreal and Oswego were, prior to the late 1900s, historically the points where these cargoes were transferred from the lakeboats and sent east by canal barge or railroad. Overseas grain cargoes were also transferred from lakers and shipped out toward the east. Thus it was almost unheard of for a load of corn to be shipped in the other direction from Oswego to Toronto. This was so much the case in 1919 that when the *Warren* departed Oswego with her load of corn, the local marine reporter simply listed her in his column as carrying coal, her normal west-bound cargo.

Sailing aboard the *Warren*, as with many small wooden lakeboats of her breed, was largely a family affair. Serving aboard Captain Stocker's boat as mate was his brother George and an even larger family group was performing duties in the boat's engine room. There was Chief Engineer William Kerr, who with the captain owned shares in the boat, and under his supervision were his brothers George and Joseph, working as fireman and second engineer respectively. These two families, with Cook Patrick Howe, deckhands Stanley Foste and William Talbot comprised the crew of the *Homer Warren*. As the boat waited her turn to take on coal, Patrick Howe stood at the rail just outside the door of his galley, gazing across the river and pondering his next painting. Overhead, the fair sky misrepresented the weather pattern forming to the west, and brightened the harbor scene in a manner that he found inspiring.

More than a half century before that inspirational Saturday, the Cleveland shipyard of Peck and Masters launched the fine wooden passenger vessel *Atlantic*. The year was 1863 and the *Atlantic* embarked on a career hauling passengers and packaged cargo around the freshwater seas. Like others of her day, the boat had passenger accommodations planted atop a cavernous hold, accessed via side-ports and capped, as usual, with a bird-cage pilothouse from which the boat would be guided. Her safe operation would be overseen by a hand-carved wooden eagle mounted proudly atop the pilothouse. The single tall mast standing behind the pilothouse could be fixed with a sail to augment the *Atlantic's* steam engine.

By the turn of the century the *Atlantic's* marginal size and antiquated accommodations had banished her to the lay-up wall. It was then that the wizard of wooden lakeboats, James Davidson, contracted her for conversion to a lumber-carrier. At Mr. Davidson's West Bay City yard the tired old *Atlantic* had her passenger quarters stripped, her sides brought up a foot and a half, the beam widened two feet and hull configured for lumber and general bulk cargos. She sailed from Bay City sporting the typical lumber hooker profile and a new name, *Homer Warren*. Shortly thereafter, the *Warren* was wed to the three-masted 170-foot schooner-barge *Ida Keith*. On October 26th, 1902, the pair were in Bay City, this time after being sold at the U.S. Marshal's auction to James Davidson, and from then on they seemed forever to be related to the

Saginaw River area. For years, the pair was seen on the lakes as steamer and consort. In the spring of 1919, Toronto vesselman J.P. Milnes engaged the *Warren* and brought her to Lake Ontario, to serve in the shuttling of coal between Oswego and Toronto.

Making frequent trips, the *Warren's* routine allowed her crew to plan around the schedule in much the same way as a passenger boat. This was a luxury that many who sailed the lakes were not afforded, but as people are want to do, they soon took the *Warren's* routine for granted. On this, the last Saturday in October, Chief Kerr had counted on the steamer getting away with her cargo in the first hours of Saturday morning, putting them in Toronto about 22 hours later. Plenty of time to grab a little sleep, muster his brothers from the boat and help his wife move their possessions while the *Warren* was unloading. Unfortunately for the chief, his well-informed plans were run aground, as Saturday dawned and the *Warren* sat waiting at the dock. After a brief conference with First Mate George Stocker, it became clear to the chief that the *Warren* might be delayed until Wednesday morning. Considering this, Captain Stocker told his good friend Chief Kerr to catch the train to Toronto and if he could get back before the *Warren* sailed, fine. If not, the boat would surely survive one trip across the lake with only two Kerrs aboard. With the prodding of the ship's officers, the chief hurried off for the Toronto train.

Monday evening found the *Warren* short one hand, Chief Kerr. Fortunately, the hiring of temporary crewmen along the Oswego waterfront in 1919 was quite easy and shortly Second Engineer Joseph Kerr had rounded up two able bodies for the *Warren's* firehold on the trip to Toronto. The dock workers that evening had overheard one of the two men give his name simply as "Thompson" and nobody could recollect the name of the other man. With a crew of eight the *Warren* was considered fully staffed, although the crew was about half of most vessels of her class. In these days before seaman's unions and regulated working shifts, many of the crew would have to pull double duty, but the boat would make money.

Shortly before four o'clock Tuesday morning, the wooden laker *Homer Warren* took up her lines and headed out onto Lake Ontario. With Captain Stocker standing in command of the pilothouse and his brother George trading his duty of first mate to take his turn as wheelsman, the steamer was soon clear of the river channel and in deep enough water to turn on the normal track for Toronto. Picking up the normal loaded pace of just over six miles-per-hour, it took less than an hour before the *Warren's* lights had been swallowed up in pre-dawn blackness. Should the schedule be kept, the *Warren* would be delivering her cargo and picking up her absent engineer in just under 24 hours.

With the rising sun, came the rising winds from Lake Ontario. As the businessmen around Oswego turned their "closed" signs around to the "open" side, they were met with a truly foul day. Along the river the vesselmen put out extra lines and braced for some stiff weather, which was exactly what they would get. No sooner had this stormy business day started, than the telegraph at the Parsons ship chandlery began clicking feverishly. The wire was from Chief Kerr in Toronto, asking if the *Warren* had departed yet and stating if she had not, he could be in Oswego by evening to re-join the crew. Mr. Parsons wired back a brief response stating that the *Warren* had sailed and that a storm was blowing at Oswego. Receiving the reply, Chief Kerr returned to his residence, planning to meet the boat Wednesday morning while she was unloading.

Apple farmers along Lake Ontario's southern shore, many of whom had yet to bring in a substantial portion of their crop, witnessed the autumn winds blast through their orchards. The furious torrents of frigid wind ripped the unharvested fruit from the trees and finished the harvest for the farmers. Throughout the morning, the low gray sky boiled with dark clouds racing southward off the lake as the wind continued to howl with increasing temper.

Just west of Sodus, New York, a farmer was making his way back to his house near Bear Creek, when he paused to scan the enraged lake. The normal gem-blue color had been replaced with storm cloud gray and the rolling surface had taken on the image of broken glass, as sharp, heaving waves jutted toward the sky. Along the beach, big breaking seas pounded the sand, the whole scene was fearful. To the west on the ill-defined horizon, an object became clear among the peaks of the seas, and caught the farmer's eye. It was a lakeboat headed east toward either Sodus Bay or Oswego. As he watched the shadowy image spewing streaks of smoke from her funnel, it is likely that the farmer felt a bit of pity for those aboard her, tossed by the lake. Turning his back to the wind and trudging toward his own doorstep, he probably could not understand why someone would want to make a living out on that lake. Opening his door, the farmer had the distinct impression that he heard the repeated toots of a distant steam whistle, but between the wind whipping the brim of his hat and the roar of the surf, it was hard to tell. Glancing at the kitchen clock, he took notice that it was just after 10 o'clock and knowing he had much to do, the farmer pushed his way back outside. At that moment he glanced back toward the lake and noticed that the lake-boat was nowhere to be seen. As he went about his chores through the stormy day, the disappearance of the steamer and that faint whistle nagged at him.

At Ogdensburg, New York, the storm interrupted the normal ferry service across the lake and at Cape Vincent the dock was completely swallowed by the in-rolling waves. In that same city Coon's big riverside warehouse was set upon by the seas that reached half-way up the four-story structure, shattering windows and sloshing through doorjambs. Much of the cheese that was stored in the building was tainted by the intruding lake and subsequently turned into a smelly moldy slime. Out at the Cape breakwater more than a dozen lakers were shielding themselves from the waves. And so it went through the night, but by dawn the storm eased and Lake Ontario began to subside.

Early Wednesday morning the phone at the J.B. McMurrich Coal Company rang, splitting the early morning hush. It was the Coast Guard calling from Sodus. Apparently guardsmen had found two bodies and a large clutter of wreckage strewn along the west side of Sodus Point. The two floaters were wearing life preservers marked *"City of Grand Rapids"* on one side and *"Homer Warren"* on the other. The word of this baffling puzzle spread wildly around the Oswego riverfront, but marine men in the know quickly pointed out that the only *City of Grand Rapids* was currently sailing for the Graham & Morton fleet out on Lake Michigan. Apparently, the life belts found on the drowned crewmen were second-hand equipment, from a former boat of the same name. There was little doubt that the bodies and the wreckage were from the *Warren*.

Once again, a wire was dispatched from Mr. Parsons to the Milnes Coal Company of Toronto regarding the *Warren*. Just as the wire was received, Chief Kerr shuffled casually into the office to inquire as to the delay in his boat's arrival. He had fully expected to see her at the coal dock. The ashen faces in the office told him in an instant that something was wrong. With a trembling hand, Mr. Milnes passed the telegraph message to the frightened chief engineer who read it and collapsed.

More word was received from Sodus Wednesday evening. At three o'clock that afternoon Lake Ontario surrendered two more bodies and from the papers in their pockets they were positively identified as the Kerr brothers, George and Joseph. Together at the end, they had come ashore surrounded by bits and pieces of the *Warren*, including a sea-chest, some pictures and some broken oars. Receiving this word, Chief Kerr and Mr. Milnes boarded the train for Oswego to bring home their people.

Through the night, flotsam washed ashore, along Sodus Point and as far west as Pultneyville. Oars, pieces of the *Warren's* pilothouse, a refrigerator, a shattered lifeboat with a hole in it, all were tossed onto the beach in the same area as the four luckless crewmen. Shortly after the wreckage washed up, the winds shifted to blowing from the south, preventing any further debris from coming in off the seas. Evidently Lake Ontario was going to keep the rest of the *Homer Warren* for herself.

Chief Kerr arrived at Oswego's North & Mitchell undertakers with Mr. Milnes and Coroner W.J. Nepham and local investigators J.B. McMurrich and Captain Le Beau. All were present to identify remains and personal effects, and to attempt to form some impression about what happened to the *Warren*. Both Chief Kerr and Mr. Milnes identified two of the sailors as the Kerr boys and another as the captain's brother George Stalker. The final body was that of artist and cook, Patrick Howe. All bodies were badly bruised, mute evidence of a violent end.

Once the investigators were past the sorrowful task of body identification, they set themselves to solving the riddle of the *Warren's* loss. The Bear Creek farmer's account of an unidentified lakeboat that was there and then gone with faint distress signals, had run in the "Oswego Daily Palladium" Wednesday evening and the investigators had the newspaper at hand. Another piece of the puzzle was a watch, worn by one of the sailors, that had stopped at 10 o'clock. Using that, along with the holed lifeboat, the marine men surmised that the *Warren*, after departing Oswego, turned on her westward course and was making good time until the storm overtook her. Something happened then to put the boat at a disadvantage against the weather and Captain Stalker was forced to turn and run before the winds toward the shelter of Sodus Bay, a shelter that he never reached. That "something" would remain a mystery until the year 2003.

In modern times we can look back across the decades and do some surmising of our own. Figuring time, speed and distance between the boat's departure and the stopped watch, as well as projecting the turn and the farmer's sighting, the boat was making about six miles-per-hour or better "over the bottom speed." This was a healthy speed for a fully-loaded wooden lakeboat of the *Warren's* class in good weather, let alone into the face of an October gale. If the storm was taking advantage of the *Warren*, it was not doing so until shortly before the captain made his turn to run. Also, whatever happened allowed at least enough time for some of the crew to secure lifejackets around themselves. The logical scenario would have Captain Stalker driving the boat full ahead into the growing storm, when suddenly her 56-year old seams began to work and leak. His only option at that point would be to run for shelter. With things looking hopeless, her crew would have mustered to abandon ship, donned lifebelts and started the boats over the side. Since the *Warren's* whistle was heard until about 10 o'clock (and that is the time that all evidence shows she went down) it is probable she had steam to the end and thus would be flooded forward. Picked up by a following sea and down by the head, her cargo forced her forward and the *Homer Warren* took a nose-dive from beneath those struggling to abandon her. Bodies are pummeled, lifeboats beaten and the whole matter is settled in seconds.

One probable answer to the end of the *Homer Warren* was discovered when the wreck itself was discovered. As the years passed and the *Warren* lay resting in her watery grave, new technologies were developed. Robert Goddard developed the liquid fueled rocket, Wernher von Braun and a team of German engineers developed that into their V-2 rocket as World War II declined and on October 4, 1957 the Soviet Union used a liquid fueled rocket to launch the world's first satellite. By then engineers had taken the science fiction idea of geo-synchronous orbital satellites and in just a few years turned the concept into reality. This all led to liquid fueled rockets launching satellites to hover high overhead which could not only transmit and receive communications, but could also triangulate locations on the ground with pin-point accuracy. Additionally, the technology of side-scan sonar was developed and became a tool for locating and identifying objects laying deep under water.

The final link in the technology chain that would string its way down to the *Homer Warren* was mixed gas SCUBA diving. This method of mixing oxygen, helium, and nitrogen allows an expert SCUBA diver to go down to depths of over 350-feet and return with all of their brain cells reasonably intact. All that was now needed to solve the *Warren's* mystery was a person with the will to do so- enter, Jim Kennand. With the help of his wife Marilyn, Kennand started hunting the *Warren* in 1978, but soon found that civilization had not yet gotten to the point where a target as illusive as the *Homer Warren* could be found and documented. He would have to wait until the next century. By 2002, all of the tools were in place. The satellites of the Global Positioning System, or GPS were hovering 22,400 miles overhead, side-scan sonar was in the digital age and both technologies were affordable and available. He also teamed up with expert diver Dan Scoville who was adept at using mixed gasses and well able to dive beyond the limits of recreational SCUBA divers. Yet even with all of these tools and all of their skill, it still took nearly two years for them to find the *Warren*. After combing more than 30 square miles of Lake Ontario they finally found the boat in very deep water.

Finding the target is one thing, but making sure that blob on the sonar screen is the *Homer Warren* is another matter. Scoville would have to go down and visit the

This is some of the actual corn cargo that was found in the wreck of the Homer Warren. *Photo courtesy Jim Kennand*

wreck. For this deep dive mixed gasses would be required. The objective was simple, identify the wreck. Although the remains fit the *Warren*, what was found in the hold was about to solve one mystery and start another. Making his way along the hull Scoville discovered tortured timbers that had been sprung outward. Moving to the spardeck, he reached into the hold expecting to pull out a handful of coal, what all of the newspapers back in 1919 had said she was carrying; instead, he got corn. It is the corn, however, that explains that "something" that happened to the *Homer Warren*. When a shipment of corn is wetted in a boat's cargo hold, that corn begins to expand like a dried sponge that suddenly has water dribbled onto it. The expansion is great as each kernel can grow to more than twice its original size. Lake water mixed with such a cargo can expand to the point where it actually forces the boat's timbers to spring outward turning a seaworthy wooden vessel into a heavily weighted basket.

Once this process started, the *Homer* would have left just enough time for her crew to get their lifejackets on before she plunged into the depths with them still scrambling for their lives. Of course, the new question now was, "why corn?" going the wrong way, west to Toronto? The normal movement of any sort of grain cargo, such as corn, on the Great Lakes is always from west to east. All of the growing areas are to the west of the lakes and all of the consuming areas are to the east. Moving any sort of grown cargo to the west is more than unusual, it is nearly unheard of! So why was the *Homer Warren* engaged in moving corn in the totally wrong direction?

One likely answer to this new question involves a few scenarios, all of which revolve around the current events of that exact period in time and an amendment to the Constitution of the United States which ushered in the mistake known as "Prohibition." Corn has always been widely used in the making of whisky. It is a bulk commodity that is highly perishable and was brokered as a key element in the brewing process in the eastern USA prior to prohibition. It is likely that the *Warren* may have arrived in Oswego with a cargo of corn. If so, the brokers in the port, knowing that if the Volstead Act, which would implement the ban on importation, manufacture or selling of alcoholic drink, was about to be passed, may not have been willing to take a load of a commodity whose value was about to crash. In this case they may have asked the vessel not to unload until they knew if the Congress would override President Wilson's veto of the Volstead act. That override came in two lopsided votes on two different days with the House voting 175 to 55 in favor of prohibition on the 27th and the Senate voting 65 to 20 in favor of prohibition on the 28th. The Volstead act took effect immediately and not only put every brewery, malt house, distiller and tavern out of business instantly, but dropped the bottom out of commodities such as corn that were used in making alcoholic drinks. It should be remembered at this point in our story that when Captain Stocker gave Chief Kerr permission to leave the boat and go back to Toronto he told him that the boat would be delayed in Oswego until at least Wednesday the 29th, the day after the final vote. If the *Warren* had come in with corn, it would be logical for her to get stuck with it following the vote.

Another scenario would have the *Warren* arriving to take coal, and suddenly discovering that the local elevators in Oswego were dumping corn stock-piles at fire-sale prices. Considering that distilling in Toronto was about to boom, because folks from the states would now have to go to Canada to buy a drink, the Canadian demand for that commodity would be about to quickly rise as would the price. It would not take much business sense to decide to change the *Warren's* regular cargo from coal to corn on the spot. A view of the lopsided vote in the house may have been enough for him to decide to load and depart earlier than Wednesday. He may have also been watching his barometer and, seeing the approaching gale, decided not to wait for the vote in the Senate. Although these are just two suppositions as to why the *Homer Warren* was carrying corn the wrong way, they go a long way toward explaining the mystery. Unfortunately, as of this writing no records detailing the *Warren's* inbound cargo have been uncovered, so this remains a supposition.

On October 28th, 1919, a man known only as "Thompson" and another who will forever remain anonymous, were lost to Lake Ontario aboard the *Homer Warren*. In the days that followed the *Warren's* loss, many a vesselman visited the Parsons store, some to buy an item or two or perhaps to send a wire, but most were there to see a painting that was on prominent display. It was a simple painting of the Oswego River, painted by a simple cook who shortly thereafter sailed to his doom aboard the *Homer Warren*, artist Patrick Howe. On May 14, 1940, John S. Parsons passed away and his collection of art was donated to the Oswego Historical Society. In the decades that followed, volunteer members of the Society fell into the casual habit of borrowing an item or two for display in their homes and businesses, normally returning the piece, but sometimes forgetting their obligation to preservation. In the 1960s this practice was halted and the Society's collection was finally secured. Today, among the hundreds of watercolors, oils and pictures, there are no images of the Oswego River signed by anyone named Howe. The artist's work, like Patrick Howe himself, has been lost. Perhaps like the two unknown crewmen, the painting is just unsigned and misplaced.

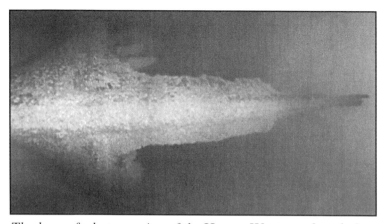

The bow of what remains of the Homer Warren - *deep below the surface of Lake Ontario. Composite image provided by Jim Kennand*

It is said that when an artist dies, his or her works become highly valuable. If that is so, then there is a work of great value and historical significance that could be just "floating" around out there someplace. If the readers of this story should find themselves in the eastern Lake Ontario area, they may want to look more carefully when cleaning that basement or attic, or when shopping at that consignment ship, Goodwill store, yard or estate sale, or perhaps in their own living room. Look for the 1919 painting signed by Patrick Howe, and bring it to the Oswego Historical Society. It is the last painting of his life and it may be, like the *Homer Warren* once was, out there somewhere waiting to be found.

DRAGON SLAYING

In the days of knights in armor many a tale of a brave knight riding through the country side and encountering a dragon were told. Proving his valor the knight did battle with the dragon and killed the beast while at the same time saving a damsel in distress or perhaps an entire village that had been terrorized by the creature. Each time that brave knights gathered such tales were exchanged and embellished. Dragons flew and had breath of fire and other powers, only the bravest and most valued of warriors could vanquish them. Since that was the case, then surely the local sovereign could not do without lots of knights because any reduction in that force would likely cause his kingdom to be overrun with dragons! Of course there are no such things as fire-breathing dragons, but in the Middle Ages who was going to know that? Most of the population was illiterate and their greatest source of information was simple word-of-mouth. Thus if some idle knight was traveling through the country side looking for an adventure that would help justify his position and status, yet finding nothing at all adventuresome along the way- a good story of slaying a dragon always did the trick. It was a lease on job security, which was cheap, simple and hard to refute. Centuries later another form of dragon slaying would become popular on the Great Lakes in the ranks of the United States Life Saving Service, also known as the USLSS.

The Life Saving Service came into being by way of the fact that most shipwreck victims perished within 200 yards of dry land. On the *Atlantic* seaboard as early as 1789 shacks containing lifeboats for breaching the surf were established. Local volunteers served as the crews. By 1874 an official US Government Life Saving Service was established and in 1876, permanent life saving "stations" were established along the shores of US waters and were staffed by highly trained crews whose job it was to watch for vessels and persons in distress and then go to their rescue.

Over the next two decades the numbers of these stations grew steadily as did the success of the Life Saving Service. Still, as with any government sponsored agency from today's NASA to history's Life Saving Service there is constant pressure from the near-sighted politicians who hold the purse strings to justify your existence on an annual basis. It does not matter if you have surveyed distant planets or saved hundreds of lives the year before, all the bean counters see is what have you done this year that will persuade them to fund you for another year. So it was that even though the Life Saving Service was showing steadily increasing success in saving human lives and valuable property, the pressure was always there for the service to justify its existence to Congress. Each year an annual report to Congress had to be submitted detailing the USLSS's activity. At first the reports were very brief, highlighting only the actions that involved the loss of life or major shipwrecks. Even that information was submitted in a very clinical and report-like manner. The fact was that the majority of the time, the storm warriors of the Life Saving Service spent their days drilling and practicing and keeping an eye out toward the water. Activity that some in Congress may look at as "just sitting around." From that point of view, why should the tax payers pay for manned stations where people sit around and wait for a shipwreck? Although it was never spoken in the service ranks, the outbreak of such thinking by the politicians was always in the thoughts of those who believed in and made their careers in the United States Life Saving Service. This was especially so at the very top where General Superintendent Sumner I. Kimball kept his finger on the pulse of the organization. One ingenious solution to this problem inadvertently gave seed to the growth of another crafty solution.

Since Kimball was required to submit annual reports to Congress, he figured this to be his annual chance to not only justify his service's existence, but to also enhance its stature. Enter William D. O'Connor as the Assistant General Superintendent. It was O'Connor's job to write the annual reports, but he was not a bureaucrat nor a bean-counter, he was in fact a former newspaper writer. O'Connor, being a professional writer, had the ability to state the facts surrounding every station's actions with words of flair that got the reader's attention without over dramatizing the facts. Beginning in 1879 the "Annual Reports" went from being a liability to the service to being their best public relations tool. Rather than focusing on how many hammers and ropes a station had, the people holding the purse strings were taken on a written adventure with station crews wherein every item was accounted for. No action was too small for O'Connor's reports either. From a lost lifebelt to a used Coston signal, every action taken by a surfman that needed to be accounted for had a story behind it and O'Connor saw to it that the Congress was fed every morsel of it.

It was this level of exposure that lead to some interesting events that we can now speculate upon. The question comes up that if your station is not experiencing any action, a good way to show that you are relevant is to go out and make some action. Of course no one would go out and create a shipwreck- so what then to do? Surfmen each night walked what was called "Beach Patrol," a lonely two to three mile stroll along a darkened beach on the lookout for vessels in distress or in danger. Upon any such discovery, the surfman was to signal the vessel. If the vessel was a wreck the surfman was then to return to the station and sound the alarm. If the vessel was heading into danger, but was warned away by his signal, the surfman was to return to the station after finishing his patrol and report the incident where it would be officially logged. The device used to signal or warn vessels was called a "Coston signal." Named for the inventor of the burning portion of the signal, Benjamin Franklin Coston, the device was designed in the late 1850s. Similar to a modern road flair, the Coston consisted of a wooden handle with a socket on one end and a spring plunger on the other. A Coston charge is loaded into the socket and then by striking the plunger the signal is ignited. It can be seen for up to 20 miles and burns for about two minutes. It was a handy device that soon became a staple of the Life Saving Service and every beach patrol carried a couple. Soon, reports began to show up where surfmen out alone on patrol were returning and reporting they had used one of their signals to warn an unknown vessel from danger. This was acceptable because in the darkness or fog a surfman could only see a vessel's lights and had no way of knowing what vessel it was. The action was logged, went into the annual report and the station got credit for preventing a shipwreck. All for the price of a Coston charge.

The first such warning of an unknown vessel shows up on October 30, 1879 "Station #9 Fifth district VA-"At 8:40 pm the patrol of the No. 9 Fifth district, saw a vessel approaching the shore, apparently steering directly for the beach. He burned his Coston light, and the vessel, heeding the warning, kept off." The next appears 21 days later, "At 3 am the patrol of station No.

14, Sixth district, North Carolina, saw a schooner in the breakers near shore, a short way beyond the patrol beat. He at once burned his Coston signal, which was answered by a fog horn from the schooner, which lowered its mainsail and headed off." In all, that annual report lists exactly eight such events. Exactly one year later, the number of those reports of "unidentified vessel" warned from danger with Coston signals doubled. By 1902 the number of vessels "warned from danger" was 237 service wide.

Keeping in mind that only a small percentage of United States coastline was patrolled by the Life Saving Service, the tally of 237 vessels warned from danger by the patrols seems to indicate that in places that were not covered, thousands of vessels should have come to grief. Statistically, the shores should be littered with wrecks where there were no life saving station patrols.

In retrospect we have to ask, just how many of those signals burned actually turned a vessel away from heading directly into the danger of shore or a reef in the vicinity of the patrol and in the immediate vicinity of the patrolman? The odds are that although a few vessels were warned in this manner each year, by 1902 most of these Coston signals were burned simply to boost the station's action numbers. Much like slaying dragons, warning a phantom vessel from danger, the firing of a Coston signal during a lonely patrol on a foggy night could often turn into an inexpensive, yet officially documented save of property and lives that only the annual report's reader could imagine. Although the life savers normally performed near super human efforts when shipwrecks happened, from lifesavers to knights in armor, even heroes are often asked by those in political control to justify their existence. The difference being that when a knight of old vanquished a dragon he only needed to bring back a story- when a Life Saving Service patrolman warned a vessel from danger, he had to bring back a burned out Coston signal.

BACK FROM
THE DEAD

As Captain Williams watched the steering pole of his vessel finally pointing toward the wide open expanse of Lake Huron, he breathed a sigh of relief. The shallows of the St. Clair and Detroit rivers were finally behind him and he would not have to fret about the low water levels of the Great Lakes again until reaching the Saint Marys River on his way up to the Soo. Of course the depths of the water up there had tended to dip below 14-feet in some cases as well. So low were the current water levels that many a Great Lakes freighter had recently snagged the bottom and nearly every lakeboat of any size was now forced to take on a lesser cargo and thus earn a lesser pay in order to avoid thumping on the bottom. Shipping company managers were chewing their fingernails to nubs over the current low water levels. Newspapers reported that it seemed as if "the bottom is dropping out of the lakes." Unseasonably warm conditions protracted into the autumn and followed a drought that had been experienced lakes-wide. In the harbor at Buffalo, New York, the high water datam had been established back in 1838 and that point was marked as "zero" on the pole set out in Lake Erie. For a decade and a half the lake level remained at an average of 2.34-feet below that high water datam. The year before this dry autumn the level was down to 3.48-feet. By mid summer it was down to 3.54-feet and just weeks before as Captain Williams had sweated out his down-bound passage the levels were measured at 4.31-feet.

Today, as his boat began her run up Lake Huron, the levels on that same Buffalo meter had dropped to a frightening 4.51-feet below the zero point. At the Detroit yacht club, one of the club stewards, Matt Kramer, saw a small island suddenly appear out of the river above the Belle Isle Bridge as the water dropped. He never knew that this low spot existed before, so he rowed out, planted an American flag on it and claimed it as his own. Elsewhere around the lakes, some speculated that the lakes may be drying up completely. The media warned that these were the lowest levels of the lakes in "history." Indeed some sort of massive, disastrous climate change must be taking place. Of course this would all sound very much like something you may hear about the lakes in 2007. "Global Warming" being the popular catch phrase for this occurrence and anthropogenic, or man-made, climate change being the reason. Captain Williams, however, was not standing watch in his pilothouse in 2007. Rather he was doing his duty as captain of the Wilson Line lakeboat *Missoula* 112 years earlier- it was Saturday, October 26, 1895.

Just over 30 hours after clearing the St. Clair River, Captain Williams was once again at his post in the *Missoula's* pilothouse. This time he was guiding her up the Saint Marys River- at night. With every turn he expected to feel the bottom reach out and take rude advantage of the *Missoula's* wooden bottom. The best that he could do was to keep his searchlight on the move and take each turn as they came. It was a tense night made worse by the low water levels, but by dawn the *Missoula* was approaching the Soo. Ahead of her was the spanking new steel steamer *Globe*. Both vessels lined up for the narrow entrance of the Canadian lock where they would lock through upbound, in tandem.

Constructed at the Quayle's Cleveland shipyard in 1887, the *Missoula* was a typical bulk carrier of her day. Measuring 272-feet long 40-feet in beam and 21-feet in depth she was steam powered and propeller driven. Her hull was made of heavy oak timbers and by every consideration she was a big seaworthy and hard working lakeboat. As her crew tossed lines to the lock wall and the gates closed behind her, the *Missoula* hissed like a giant wooden workhorse chomping at the bit to resume her toil and not at all pleased to be forced to stop and wait for the lock to fill. In less than 40 minutes her wish was granted and the gates ahead opened. Out of the lock the *Globe* churned and in her wake huffed the *Missoula*. There was no more worry about low water levels in the *Missoula's* pilothouse. Ahead lay nothing but deep, deep water and in another day and a half, she would be in Port Arthur taking on her downbound load of 70,000 bushels of Manitoba wheat. It was just after 10 o'clock on a glorious autumn morning as the boat departed the Canadian lock with the word that they would be back downbound by Saturday.

Amid the clamor of the industrial heartbeat that was Sault Saint Marie in 1895, the comings and goings of vessels were almost too numerous to keep track of. It was an era when most communication was done by telegraph and word of mouth. Vessel comings and goings were at the authority of the captain alone and often his on-the-spot decisions could drastically alter a vessel's planned schedule. Perhaps that is why the *Missoula* was not missed until she was three days overdue at the locks. Telegraphs clicked urgently at both the Soo and at Port Arthur all day Monday November 4th, and the confirmation was made certain-the *Missoula* had left the ports of Port Arthur and Fort William with a cargo of grain at nine o'clock Thursday evening. She should have locked down at the Soo late Friday or before dawn on Saturday, but she had not.

A respectable southwest gale had blown across Lake Superior late Friday and into Saturday and some ashore believed this may have led to something happening to the vessel. Speculation was that perhaps she had run for shelter and was aground in some remote location on the north shore. Perhaps she had run into mechanical problems and was simply delayed in her arrival. Most, however, had the nagging feeling that the *Missoula* had become another name on Lake Superior's roll-call of ships gone missing and she, along with her crew, would never again be seen at the Soo. Such was not uncommon it this era on the Great Lakes. The modern shipwreck database is peppered with the names of vessels that simply sailed out and never returned. When such events take place the spectators are always divided into the hopeful and the hopeless. As time passes, the ranks of those hopeful for the *Missoula* steadily began to shrink.

Word of the missing *Missoula* rapidly spread from the Soo to Duluth, Port Huron, Buffalo and other port cities around the Great Lakes. By the time the newspapers were reporting the boat as being 85 hours overdue, the ranks of those who expected her and her crew to come in off the lake had dwindled to almost no one. For two days every downbound lakeboat had been asked if any sign had been seen of the *Missoula*. All of them replied that they had seen nothing- not a trace at all.

Dispatched from the Soo on Monday, a search party sailed out onto Lake Superior to try and solve the growing mystery of the *Missoula*. Three steamers set out on three different tracks. The steamer *Telegram* was assigned to run along the south shore and look for any sign of the missing lakeboat. The tug *Booth* was to sail in and out of the countless little bays along the shore and the steamer *Olympia* was to back-track the outside passage to Port Arthur. Since Friday's gale the weather had remained good and it was speculated that there had been plenty of time for the crew to have found a way to civilization had they survived the boat's demise. Now gruesome speculation of the boat having caught fire and burned to the waterline with her crew aboard was being tossed about. Of course the fact that such a fire would have been visible for miles, even in Friday's gale, was handily overlooked. Another popular notion was that the boat had been blown to the north shore and struck a rock causing her to founder quickly in deep water with all hands. On Tuesday the steamer *Telegram* arrived back from her search and reported no sign of the *Missoula*.

On Wednesday morning a telegraph message was sent from Captain Hursley of the tug *Booth*. He too had found nothing in his search, although he had only gotten as far toward Port Arthur as Port Caldwell before Lake Superior became temperamental and caused him to take shelter there. Although that was about three quarters of the way to Port Arthur, and well beyond the point where the *Missoula* could likely have been blown ashore, he still stated that he would continue his search as soon as the weather allowed. The *Olympia* arrived at Fort William and reported seeing not a trace of the missing *Missoula*. Down in Cleveland, Captain Thomas Wilson, owner and manager of the *Missoula,* told the news media that he had not given up any hope that the boat would not be found safe with her crew alive. The ever skeptical, the news report then added that other "Vessel owners here, however, do not share his confidence."

Just as the word was circulating around the Soo that the three search vessels had found nothing, the telegraph began ticking with renewed urgency. The message was sent from Port Arthur. It was the word that would make even Captain Thomas Wilson's confidence shrink. The package freighter *Arabian* had just arrived in Port Arthur from Michipicoten Island on her regular supply run. When steaming out of the harbor on the south side of the island her crew had spotted a large quantity of wreckage washing up on the south side of what was called "Little Long Island." This appeared to be the white cabins of a large steamer. Only one large steamer was missing in that area and it was the *Missoula*.

Word of the discovery of the wreckage spread quickly around the Soo. Each lakeboat that tossed a line out at either the U.S. or Canadian locks was given the spoken news that the *Missoula* was now undoubtedly gone and had probably taken her entire crew with her. From Sault Saint Marie the same news was wired to all points around the Great Lakes-Superior had taken yet another laker and her crew. An atmosphere of sad inevitability settled around the Soo. That was the way of sailing the lakes in the autumn months. The *Missoula* and her crew would never again lock down many would shake their heads and say. They were all half right.

Nearly at the moment that the entire Great Lakes community had given up all hope for the crew of the *Missoula*, a tiny sailboat with five people aboard came skimming into the Soo. As if returning from a fine summer jaunt onto the blue shimmering lake, they casually sailed through Sault Saint Marie's maritime commotion. Those who recognized the men were so shocked that they froze amid whatever they were doing and simply gazed in amazement. Indeed they were looking at five ghosts back from the dead- it was Captain Williams and four of his crew!

Again the word flashed around the Soo like a lightening strike. In no time at all Captain Morton of the Wilson line came dashing down to the locks where the five castaways were being mobbed by everyone wanting to know how they had escaped Superior's death grip. Captain Williams refused to give any information other than to say that the rest of his crew were safe at Lizard Island. He had also ordered all of those with him to not say a word about what had happened to the *Missoula*- that is... if they wanted to remain employed with Wilson Marine. Of course it is pretty easy to keep your crew quiet when they are standing there flanked by the captain and a big wig of the shipping company. That power fades quickly, however, and by the time that the entire crew had been transported down to Port Huron, some voices were talking fairly freely and the local media were eating it up.

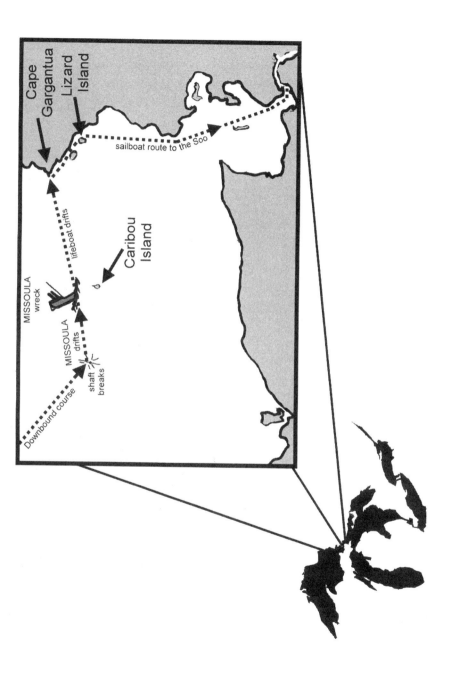

Cape Gargantua

Lizard Island

sailboat route to the Soo

Caribou Island

lifeboat drifts

MISSOULA wreck

MISSOULA drifts

shaft breaks

Downbound course

With a full load of Canadian grain in her belly the *Missoula* departed Port Arthur at nine o'clock Thursday night. She was running her usual course toward the Soo when, in the early hours of Friday morning, her propeller shaft suddenly snapped. This shaft was a thick-walled steel pipe about as big around as a telephone pole and to have one snap was not unheard of. There would, however, be no way to repair it. Such repair would require dry docking and removal of the entire shaft. The problem now was that without any form of communication, the crew had no way to call for help- they could do nothing other than to sit and wait for a passing vessel to spot them and render assistance. Adding to their dilemma was the fact that a strong southwest wind was beginning to blow. A wind from that direction would soon blow the powerless lakeboat out of the common shipping lanes and into a part of Lake Superior where almost no one navigated. As the winds grew to gale force, the waves grew as well and soon the helpless *Missoula* was far from the shipping lanes and rolling on her beam ends. For more than 24 hours she wallowed in the sea troughs until just before nine o'clock on Saturday morning. It was then that her cargo of grain shifted and set the boat hard on her beam with her rail beneath the water. Now the lake began to flood her hold and it became clear that the *Missoula* was doomed. Captain Williams gave the order for his crew to take to the boats and abandon the *Missoula*.

Lowering the first of the *Missoula's* lifeboats, the vessel's crew watched in horror as the little boat was quickly swamped and swallowed by Lake Superior. Keenly learning from their first attempt, they launched the second, and only remaining lifeboat. This time the little boat remained afloat and the entire crew of 17 mariners scrambled aboard. They pushed off and rowed clear of the *Missoula*. Less than a half hour after they escaped the *Missoula*, the castaways watched their boat go down, bow-first, and vanish into the depths of Lake Superior. Surrounded by the endless churning lake and peppered by blowing snow, the survivors could do nothing more than drift with the winds. All day Saturday and through the night the castaways drifted in the bitter cold wind and stinging spray and snow. Their ordeal went on through most of Sunday until land appeared in the distance. By Sunday evening they dragged their lifeboat onto the Canadian dry land at Cape Gargantua. It was then decided to build a camp and a large fire and wait until morning before proceeding any farther. Even in modern times, this part of the Lake Superior shore is a remote wilderness consisting of ice-age finger lakes and juts of land preserved as the Lake Superior Provincial Park. When the crew of the *Missoula* landed there, it was nearly as inhospitable as the surface of the lake. Although there was no danger of drowning, there was the added danger of becoming dinner for the local bears and wolves. The best bet for the crew was to build a large fire, dry off and then head down along the shore in the morning.

Daylight revealed Lake Superior as being much more calm than the night before and once more the crew of the *Missoula* took to their lifeboat and headed south. Traveling a dozen miles down the lake shore they came upon the fishing village at Lizard Island. The fishermen took the castaways in, fed them and loaned Captain Williams a small sailing boat. Using that, he was able to make the 65 mile trip down to Sault Ste. Marie and return from the dead. A steamer was sent to Lizard Island to pick up the remaining crew and the adventure came to an end.

Among the clamor of the industrial revolution and the rapid expansion of Great Lakes maritime commerce, the story of the loss of the *Missoula* soon faded into the background and was forgotten. Her hulk rests on the bottom of Lake Superior- some speculate it is just off shore of Michipicoten Island where one of her spars was found anchored to an unknown object deep below the surface- others say she is in deep water above Caribou Island. Her story and that of her crew, however, rests right here. It is the story of one vessel that went missing on Lake Superior, and her crew- who all came back from the dead.

BETWEEN THE FLAGPOLES

It was a warm summer day in the mid 1980s- the date was July 4th and most Americans were taking the day off to relax, picnic and celebrate their liberty. The weather across the entire Great Lakes region was clear, warm and sunny. Out on the surface of the lakes, however, this Independence Day was no day-off for the vessels and mariners. Although few ashore took much notice, the lakeboats remained hard at work.

Coming off of Saginaw Bay one of the big Title XI lakers was lined up in the channel headed for the Saginaw River. Now... for the purposes of this story, the name of the vessel will remain unpublished and it must suffice to say that the events here were witnessed by the author. The vessel was a member of the American Steamship Company fleet and in her hold was a full load of coal bound for the Consumer's Power plant located at the mouth of the river. This facility provides power to the tri-cities and much of the surrounding area in mid-Michigan. As the boat slid up to the dock a well practiced routine of lines and crew going ashore began. The dock had a well leveled mesa of coal from the previous vessel's visit and now this new arrival was prepared to swing her self-unloading boom out and place her cargo on the dock. The only question was- where to put the load? The dock area there is just over 2,500-feet long and nearly 1,000-feet wide. Normally, specific loads of coal are placed in specified locations and in patterns that make it efficient for the bulldozers and spreaders to move the load to the hoppers that transport it to the plant. A dock supervisor is always on duty to show the vessel exactly how to drop the load... well, almost always.

By the time that the lakeboat's lines were made fast and the ladders were dropped ashore with their safety nets slung below, several radio calls had already been placed to the dock, but no one had responded. Additional radio calls had been placed to the Bay City Marine operator in an effort to contact the dockmaster. Soon those first few minutes at the dock began to stretch into more than an hour, yet there was no word from anyone on the dock. A crewmember was sent on foot to search for someone, anyone, who could tell them where to put the load. He came back and reported that he could find no one. Even the guard shack was vacant and the gate was chained. More radio calls went unanswered- after all, it was a holiday.

Title XI vessels were designed to be built and operated with maximum efficiency. Commonly called "River Class" or "Stem-winders" by the maritime folks, these vessels differed from the traditional Great Lakes profile. They have all of the accommodations located aft and are constructed as self-unloaders. Their holds are shaped in a hopper-like "V" so as to allow bulk cargo to slide down. In the bottom of the hold a continuous conveyor belt runs its length. Trap doors in the bottom of the hold open to allow cargo to drop onto the belt. The cargo is then dropped onto a second belt that moves it vertically where it is dumped onto a third belt that runs the length of an unloading boom. This boom, measuring about 250-feet long is swung over the dock to allow the entire burden of cargo to be off loaded at any water-side location in just a few hours. Yet even when operated at maximum efficiency these stem-winders cost, in 1980s dollars, more than $1,000 an hour to run. In order to operate at peak efficiency, however, these vessels must keep moving. They have to load, sail, arrive, unload and then move on to the next cargo- not a minute can be wasted. By mid day on that pleasant July 4th, the stem-winder that was docked at Consumer's Power had been sitting for more than four hours at an accumulated loss of more than $4000 by the time the first response to repeated phone and radio calls had been received.

It was a message from a security guard saying he was coming down to unlock the gate and that he could probably find a phone number that may help in his book at the guard shack. That was the good news; the bad news was that it may take him more than an hour to get to the dock. Of course this was a time when most telephone communications were done by way of landline rather than by cellphone. It was a time before every person walked around with a phone in their pocket or hung on their ear. That guard's off-duty effort, although above and beyond his responsibilities, would cost the vessel another $1,000 in delay.

About the time that the off-duty guard arrived to try and help, progress, of a sort, was reported from the folks at Bay City Marine radio. They had managed to get a message through to someone who could get a message to someone. Among all of this the boat's officers and captain were about ready to blow a fuse. Often, such delays are more easily understood at the time, however, at the end of the season, when the bean-counters press their sharp pencils to the ledgers or key in figures to their computers, the blame can come back and directly bite the captain. No doubt, there was some steam brewing in the pilothouse that day as everyone waited. There seemed the very real chance that no one may be there to direct the unloading until the morning of the 5th. That would equate to more than a $20,000 operational loss for this cargo and vessel.

By late afternoon the guard had arrived, found his list of emergency contact numbers and began calling. The mate of the vessel was in the guard shack with a hand-held radio to allow instant communication with the pilothouse if anyone ever answered any of the calls.

Eventually, it appeared as if this dilemma was about to come to an end as the mate radioed that they indeed had a contact. Excitedly the answer as to where to put the load was relayed. "He says, just put it between the flagpoles," came the message. In the pilothouse there was near shock looking out the windows, there was only about 300-feet between "the flagpoles" and placing the entire cargo there would result in a mountain of coal that the dock spreaders may not be able to knock down for several weeks. "Does he know we've got 28,000 tons here?" was the retort. After a brief silence the answer was repeated and relayed by the mate, "He says just put it between the flagpoles." Another long silence followed and then the word came from the pilothouse... "Oooookay."

That evening pleasure boats gathered in droves along the Saginaw River in Bay City. Along the riverbank in parks and assorted open areas people gathered as darkness fell. Everyone was looking forward to the annual spectacle of the Bay City Fireworks show. In the night the sky flashed and sparkled with the dazzle of the fireworks and the "Oooo's" and "Ahhh's" of the crowd seemed to come in unison with each burst. No one noticed the big, empty laker as she backed away from the Consumer's Power dock and out into the bay with the flashes of the fireworks reflecting in her pilothouse windows. Once in the open bay she turned and headed off leaving in her wake the fireworks, the Consumer's Power dock and two flagpoles- buried in a huge mountain of coal that would take weeks to sort out.

ICE TRAP

For two weeks the silhouettes of the stranded freighters could be seen off shore of Marquette. Miles of unrelenting and impassable ice lay between the lakeboats and the port. To make the matter worse all of these boats had been at sea for nearly a month and the word was that they had run out of food several days earlier. Of course no one but those aboard the vessels knew for certain what was the true plight of the boats and their crews. One person who did know for sure was Captain Carl Rydholm of the oreboat *Munising*. As he gazed helplessly from the boat's pilothouse and watched the dawn he knew that today would likely bring only futile decisions producing useless attempts at freeing his vessel.

The spring of 1917 was an accelerating and frightening time for most of the planet Earth. For the past three years the powers that be in Europe had been fighting a war that was rapidly spreading across all of the globe and by early 1917 the situation was rapidly escalating and threatening to pull the United States in. Canada was already involved in the war and shipping of products such as iron ore and grain was at an all time high on the Great Lakes. On the sixth day of April, the United States declared war on Germany and thousands of American men rushed to sign up and march into the human meat grinder that was being called "The war to end all wars." Before the war ended in November of 1918 deaths from war related causes would total more than 8.5 million human beings and 126,000 of those would be from the United States. This was a period of national emergency and every pound of iron ore and every bit of grain that could be shipped across the lakes in the 1917 season would be urgently needed.

Unfortunately, the preceding winter had been especially brutal. As the month of April began, the waters of the Straits of Mackinaw were choked with ice and the Saint Marys River was frozen over. Still the big lakeboats were dispatched from the lower lakes ports with orders to smash their way north to the rich iron ore waiting at Lake Superior's docks. Without regard for the bitter winter that was still gripping the upper lakes, nearly 100 lakeboats began plowing upbound. The assault on the ice of the Saint Marys River began on April 7th, when the "ice-crusher" *Algomah* began working her way upbound in the lower river. Having first been put to work cracking the ice of the Great Lakes in 1881 the 127-foot break-bulk steamer *Algomah* started her career on the Straits of Mackinaw. In her day it was thought that the best way to break ice was to give a steamer very heavy wooden hull timbers and then shape her bow so that it would ride up on the ice and crush it with her weight, thus they were at first referred to as "ice-crushers" rather than ice-breakers. The concept was correct and is still used today. The problem was that when the vessel stops moving forward it expends most of its forward inertia and then requires a huge amount of energy to again move forward. So when the ice becomes too thick for the boat to move forward and crush at the same time, it can easily become trapped in the ice. Vessels can regain forward inertia by backing and then making another forward run, but if the ice prevents sufficient backward room the ice-crusher is again trapped. Additionally, broken cakes of ice that slide into the path of a backing ice-crusher can damage or strip its propeller and leave the vessel totally helpless. In modern times all sorts of tools that people on the *Algomah* could only have dreamed of are in the ice-breaker's toolbox, but in 1917, she had only her weight and inertia. Although noted for being a good spring ice-crusher, the *Algomah* was insufficient for the task she had been designed to do which was to sail through the winter ice Straits of Mackinaw. In April of 1917, however, the quarter century old steamer was well up to the task of crushing the ice on the Saint Marys River.

Although the first boat had reached the Soo, many others would be slowed to a snail's pace by the windblown ice flows. The sheets of ice were blown into stacks called "windrows" and measuring as much as 20- to 30-feet thick. In between the windrows the surface of the lake continued to freeze as the winter temperatures refused to give way to spring. Attacking winter's grip were two of the McDougall designed whaleback steamers. The whalebacks *James B. Neilson* and *Henry Cort* temporarily traded their roles of oreboats to become icebreakers. Whalebacks were constructed with the idea that rather than fighting off the seas, if you were to welcome them aboard their very weight would stabilize the vessel. This design not only worked, but had one unexpected benefit- it made these big steel vessels terrific icebreakers. These cigar shaped steamers with their unique spoon-shaped bows had the ability to drive easily on top of the ice and then allow their own weight to crush through the frozen lake surface. In the Straits of Mackinaw, the whalebacks actually made progress- until the winds shifted. In spite of all the technology of 1917 and the best machines of the industrial revolution and while throngs of men signed up to go and fight the war that had now come to the United States, everyone on the Great Lakes had to wait for the weather to change.

By the third week in April the winter finally began to give way to spring and the temperatures began to warm while the winds began to blow in a favorable direction. The *Neilson* and *Cort* turned their spoon bows into the Saint Marys River. Behind them came a conga line of lakeboats. Bringing up the rear of that line was the steamer *Munising*. Captain Rydholm had brought her out of winter lay-up and the port of Toledo on April

18th and had found little trouble with ice on his trip. Entering the Saint Marys river he kept the *Munising* in the path that had been broken in the ice by the scores of freighters preceding him to the Soo. Launched in 1902 as the steamer *F.M. Osborne*, the 400-foot *Munising* was one of a breed of oreboats born in an era when lakeboats were expanding in size so rapidly that she was outclassed almost before she came off the builder's ways. Already on the ways were vessels of 500-feet in length and keels were being readied for 600-footers. Yet the demand for iron ore was so great in this era that the 400-footers simply went to work and earned an honest living.

In 1916 the *Osborne* was acquired by the Cleveland Cliffs Iron Company and painted their colors of black hull and pea-green cabins with white trim and renamed *Munising*. Captain Rydholm was given command of the vessel in her first season with the Cliffs- 1917. Running only in daylight it took him two days to break his way up to Sault Saint Marie and the Soo locks with the *Munising*. Once there, however, he discovered a flotilla of 77 lakeboats tied up beneath the locks like a massive steel raft. Although the lower Saint Marys river was passable, the upper river and Whitefish Bay were still blocked by heavy ice. In fact only two oreboats were allowed to enter the locks. They came from the back of the line escorted by the tug *Illinois*. They were the whalebacks *Cort* and *Neilson* and both were on their way up from Escanaba. After breaking the path that the *Munising* had sailed up in. the whalebacks were sent back to the Mackinaw straits to break a path between the lower Saint Marys River and the ore docks at Escanaba. While doing that job, however, both whalebacks had blades stripped from their propellers. The *Neilson* had just one blade stripped from her propeller, but the *Cort* was stripped of all her buckets and left with just a bare propeller shaft. By that time the winds had shifted and began blowing the ice clear of the shipping lanes so the *Neilson* took the *Cort* in tow and the two limped to the Soo. Once there, an unusual dry-docking took place. The whalebacks would be tugged, one at a time, into the Weitzel lock which was then pumped dry so that workmen could replace one of the boat's propeller blades. Following that, the lock was refilled and the whaleback would pass upbound. After that a similar process was done with the next damaged whaleback. The *Neilson* went first as her damage was limited to a single blade, a replacement for which could be obtained locally. By evening on the 25th of April she was ready to go and locked upbound then was secured above the locks to await the light of the next morning before proceeding into the fight with Whitefish Bay's ice. The *Cort*, however, was another matter as her propeller had been completely stripped away and her owners, Pittsburgh Steamship Company, would have to ship all of the parts to make up a full propeller to the Soo before she could sail again.

While the repair work on the *Neilson* was being completed, word reached the Soo from farther up along the Saint Marys River that open water could now be seen to the north. The winds had shifted and the heavy ice that the biggest boats built by humans could not overcome now seemed to be breaking up under the forces of nature. With that the freighter masters began to itch to be locked upbound. What was actually happening, of course, was the baiting and setting of Lake Superior's annual ice trap. Nearly every season since the beginning of navigation with steel-hulled steamers this same trap had been set and baited.

The big lake uses its entire expanse and sets a series of clever traps with its frozen surface, the bait being the urge of the captains to haul that first load of the season. Every year, up until the decline of shipping on the lakes in the last decades of the 20th century, vessel masters let their desire to haul cargo overcome their memory of the previous year's trappings and they sail directly into Superior's ice trap. So it was that on the 25th day of April, 1917 the lakeboats *John J. Barlum* and *Harvester* locked through and huffed upbound toward that reported open water. Both found that there was a natural channel melted in the river's ice and the winds had pushed much of the ice out of Whitefish Bay. Confidently, the two lakers plowed ahead into Lake Superior and the seemingly distant ice field. And just as quickly they became stuck in the ice flow that had blown out of Whitefish Bay and into open Lake Superior. A wireless message sent from the *Harvester* said that although both boats were in no danger, they were hopelessly stuck in ice that extended out into Lake Superior as far as the eye could see.

Although the "Steel Trust" boats of the Pittsburgh Steamship Company fleet, including the *Neilson*, were now ordered to remain at the Soo and not take the bait of the ice trap, other companies did not send such orders to their vessel masters. So the process of vessels locking upbound continued in spite of the reports from the *Harvester*. Many of the masters felt that at least getting above the locks would save time once the ice did open up. Lake Superior knew that her bait was very compelling and once above the locks the urge would soon draw more lakeboats into her icy traps.

Among those masters itching to get above the locks was Captain Rydholm who took his turn to lock the *Munising* upbound through the Poe Lock. Together with the oreboat *William Roberts*, Captain Rydholm's *Munising* was logged as passing upbound at nine o'clock on the evening of April 27th. The *Munising* then tied up above the locks to wait for the ice and weather for the next two days. By then Captain Rydholm's instincts told him it was time to start moving, so he ordered the *Munising's* lines let go from the boats he had been rafted to and began making his way upbound. Most of the other vessels, however, waited until the morning of April 30th before proceeding. It was on that morning that wireless reports from the *Harvester* were received by the fleet waiting at the Soo and reported that she and her companion, the *Barlum*, had at last found open water and that the winds were now blowing the ice toward mid lake. The word was shouted by megaphone from oreboat to oreboat and soon billows of black coal smoke and the hoots of steam whistles filled the air signaling that the 1917 shipping season on Lake Superior had begun.

While the armada of oreboats departed the Soo, Mr. C.G. Lampman, the Pittsburgh Steamship Company's local manager at Sault Saint Marie, suddenly found himself in a bit of a spot. On orders from the company headquarters he had told all of the captains of their boats that they were to remain at the Soo until conditions on Lake Superior would allow them to run cleanly all the way up to Duluth. Now he had the masters of other fleets making a mad dash upbound while nearly two score of his company's own captains were breathing fire itching to get the go ahead. It would be a full week before Mr. Lampman would be allowed to issue that release- he was in for a very long workweek indeed.

With nearly 50 lakeboats coming up behind him Captain Rydholm guided the *Munising* slowly through the remaining ice above Whitefish Point. The open waters into which he pointed the *Munising's* steering pole were, in reality, just wishful thinking. Just over the horizon to the south was a massive icepack that was anchored to the southern shore and extended more than two dozen miles into the lake. Just over the horizon to the north was an even more dangerous icepack. This one likely stretched more than 75 miles wide and was floating freely in mid-lake. The Pittsburgh Steamship

Company's management had been wise to hold their boats at the Soo, because there was no clear path across Lake Superior, there was only the jaws of this massive ice trap. As the wind blew from the northeast, it sent that giant roving icepack down to crush those lakeboats who now thought themselves to be in open water.

By the evening of the 30th of April Captain Rydholm estimated the *Munising's* position to be about 10 miles south of Caribou Island. It was then that Lake Superior sprung one of her icy traps by turning that northeast wind into a sudden northeast gale. Through the night the storm tossed the *Munising*, but everyone's mind was not on the waves and blowing snow, they were focused on the masses of ice that this blow would bring down from mid lake. There was the very real chance that windblown pack ice could smash the *Munising* and send her to the bottom. In the blackness of the night's gale with no other vessels in sight, the *Munising* could end up on that long list of vessel's gone missing on Lake Superior. Captain Rydholm ordered the boat's big searchlight to keep scanning the darkness looking for the ice flows, but none were seen. Daylight finally revealed that the huge ice flows were indeed closing in on the *Munising* as the gale continued. Now, with the help of daylight, Captain Rydholm at least could see which way to run. He turned the boat and headed due west. He had in mind that he would run before the gale and gain the lee of the Keweenaw Peninsula. By the time that the gale let up, the *Munising* was well west of her destination of Marquette. The huge icepack to the north had been blown in behind her effectively closing the door to any back-track course and the freighter found herself in a small area of open water just north of Huron Island.

Calm weather now offered Captain Rydholm his only remaining option- other than remaining anchored in his present location for the next few weeks. He would have to take on the ice and try and break his way toward Marquette. Her triple expansion steam engine provided the *Munising* with 1,310 horsepower to drive her 3,838 ton steel hull through the ice- that's less horsepower than a modern day monster truck. From the *Munising's* present position, there were more than two dozen miles of heavy ice between her and Marquette. Captain Rydholm was about to find out that the job ahead was not just difficult- it was impossible.

Modern wreck divers on Lake Superior tell of finding ice ware on wooden wrecks at depths of 100-feet. That means that the ice on that lake has at times been as thick as 100-feet. This is caused by the same windrow actions that choke the straits of Mackinaw, only on a far larger scale. Ice is piled upon itself in a near glacier fashion and forces itself to great depths. It was this sort of ice that the *Munising* was about to challenge. At first the *Munising* found the ice on the outer edge of the field to be breakable and the boat made slow progress. From May 2nd to the 6th the oreboat shoved into the ice making just a few boat lengths each day. On Sunday, the sixth day of May, 1917 the hull of the *Munising* shuddered to a stop. The ice flowed in behind her and would no longer allow her to back, and the ice ahead was too thick to let her move forward. The boat was now firmly stuck in the ice nearly a dozen miles from Marquette and nine miles from the nearest land which was Presque Isle. It was then that First Mate F. P. Bamford came to the pilothouse and informed Captain Rydholm that the boats provisions of food were running low.

Of course everyone knows that the month of May is in the season called "Spring" which is followed closely by the season known as "Summer" and ice will normally melt sometime during these two seasons. On Lake Superior, however, those seasonal rules are written a bit differently. In fact, it often seems as if Superior's winter ice may hang around into summer. In reality, even the worst ice on the big lake normally begins to fade in the first weeks of May. When you are trapped in the ice aboard a lake freighter with more than two dozen crewmen and the news comes that the food supplies are dwindling, however, even the prospect of being in that position for a few days is frightening. Captain Rydholm was beginning to wish that he had stayed at the Soo for another day.

Using one of the freighter's small wooden rowboats, the *Munising's* crew cobbled up a home-made ice-boat. Using some scrap wood they fashioned runners to allow the little craft to be pushed or dragged across ice and the fact that it was indeed a boat would, they reasoned, help them overcome any open water that they may find. First Mate Bamford and Wheelsmen Arthur

Marotki, James Deagon and George Frisch along with deckhand Salem Hamsa volunteered to take the contraption and try and make it to shore. Nearly the entire crew had mustered at the rails to watch and help as the ice-boat and the five adventurers were lowered to the frozen surface of Lake Superior.

The plight of the *Munising* had not gone unnoticed by the local folks ashore. Large crowds had gathered on the high grounds of Presque Isle's Black Rocks each day for the past several days and observation of the *Munising* had become a local pastime. Rumor had it that the food aboard the boat had probably run out days ago and the crew was now in a starving condition. Among those watching the situation was Alva Howard, a local surveyor. Alva had taken it upon himself to bring out his surveyor's tripod and transit scope and trained it upon the vessel. He had become the on-scene commentator giving play-by-play to the crowd detailing an event that literally was moving as fast as ice melting. At eight o'clock on the morning of May 7th, however, the level of excitement suddenly picked up. It was then that Alva saw the ice-boat and the five crewmen going over the side.

Although it sounds simple to take a rowboat equipped with ice runners and use it to traverse nine miles across a frozen lake, the fact is that the journey would be nearly impossible. Rather than a smooth skating surface that those not familiar with ice on the Great Lakes would envision, the surface was a nine mile long jumble of huge ice cakes, strewn and angled in every direction. In between the cakes of ice would occasionally be found open water or worse yet- slush. Each move that the men made could easily see them vanish into the frigid lake. As Alva Howard announced every step, the crowd was thrilled to hear of one man or another slipping and recovering. Eventually every one of the adventurers had taken an icy soaking and they were all still miles from shore.

Over the horizon beyond the distant *Munising* and her party of ice-traversing adventurers the silhouettes of more lakeboats began to appear. Smashing their way toward the *Munising's* location came the Cleveland Cliffs boats *Grand Island* and *Ishpeming*. Shortly after their appearance these two boats were joined by the Cliffs vessels *Peter White* and *J.H. Bartow*. All four of these boats managed to crush their way no closer to the *Munising's* position than a mile. Alva Howard announced the arrival of each of the boats and then the crowd was silenced by the haunting sound of one of the big freighters as her whistle blew a series of distress hoots. As those sounds softly echoed ashore, the drama increased.

From Marquette harbor the tug *Thompson* began smashing her way toward the stranded fleet. Aboard, the tug carried six weeks worth of provisions for the stranded mariners. Up on Presque Isle point, the crowd of shore-bound onlookers were now really getting a show. "Here comes the *Thompson!*" someone shouted as the tug headed out. It seemed as if the entire story was coming to a climax. Then the tug's progress began to slow as the black smoke from her stack belched into the air and hovered just above the frozen lake. Soon her forward gains against the ice were slowed until the *Thompson* herself became stuck firmly in Lake Superior's frozen surface. Now it looked as if the tug's crew may end up eating the provisions intended for the *Munising* while everyone waited for summer.

Also watching as the *Munising's* five man team worked their way across the ice were the Coast Guard crew at the Marquette life-saving station. Although the life-saving station was well equipped to handle any sort of shipwreck, they had no means to rescue mariners stranded across nine miles of jumbled ice. Like the boatwatchers on Presque Isle, the Coast Guardsmen could do little more than watch through a telescope.

The early morning that has witnessed the five men depart the *Munising* now stretched into a darkening evening. For 10 hours the five adventurers had kept up their painful trek across the ice. As darkness began to close in, the crew of the life-saving station had seen enough and they headed out, stretching a safety line, to meet the men of the *Munising*. Once the soaked, exhausted and benumbed team had been reached, the life-savers hurried them to the station and later transported them to the Clifton Hotel. There the five mariners were given dry clothing and hot food. They also informed the locals that, although the food aboard the *Munising* was in very short supply, the crew were not in a starving condition.

Over the next two days the crowds watching the frozen drama continued to grow. It is human nature to never allow facts to supersede a good rumor of gloom and doom, so the fact that there was no starvation taking place on the *Munising* was easily overshadowed by the rumor that the crewmen were in a state of terminal suffering and starvation. Thus when the *Ishpeming* finally made her way along side the *Munising* the crowd ashore celebrated in relief.

By May 10th, the big ore boats that had been stranded just outside of Marquette were able to make their way to the docks and restock and resume the 1917 shipping season. The *Munising* recovered her five adventurers, took on provisions and prepared to depart as local residents visited the docks and were disappointed at not seeing scenes of gruesome starvation. Out on Lake Superior the ice was rapidly breaking itself up and melting into a spring thaw. As Captain Rydholm prepared to take the *Munising* out he saw that the *Grand Island*, *Ishpeming* and *Peter White* were successfully breaking a channel into open water. This, it was later reported in the Marquette Mining Journal, had been the worst local ice jam in four and a half decades- but to the vesselmen it was just another spring breakout. By blowing the *Munising's* whistle Captain Rydholm indicated to everyone in earshot that the big drama was over and the *Munising* was simply going back to work. Still, he could not help but feel that he had been baited into one of Lake Superior's most icy traps.

GLOSSARY

Abeam - Beside or perpendicular to the side of a vessel.

Aft - Behind or to the rear of a vessel.

Aground - Running onto the bottom of shallow water.

Back Broken - A vessel's hull fails across its width.

Ballast - Something used to weigh a vessel down so that it runs lower in the water.

Barge - A vessel that is intended to move cargo without power of its own.

Bark - Usually a three masted sailing vessel with mizzenmast fore and aft rigged and the others being square rigged (also known as a Barque).

Brig - Two masted sailing vessel that is square rigged.

Bulkhead - A vertical wall that divides the hull widthwise.

Canaller - A vessel built specifically to transit the locks of the old Welland Canal.

Cut Down - To remove cabins and or decks to facilitate use of a vessel in another capacity.

Davit - The support boom normally used for swinging out and lowering lifeboats.

Donkey Boiler - Used to produce steam for uses other than propulsion, such as steering and or heating.

Fathom - Six feet.

Fire Hold - The portion of the engine room where crewmen stand and shovel coal into the furnace that heats the boilers.

Flotsam - Floating wreckage.

Fo'c'sle - The deck house built beneath the elevated portion of the bow (also known as fore-castle).

Fore and Aft Rigged - Sails set parallel or lengthwise to the hull.

Founder - To sink suddenly or disastrously.

Funnel - Smoke stack.

Gale - Winds of between 40 and 74 miles per hour.

Gunnel - (also known as gunwhales) where the boat's side meets her spar deck.

Hawser - A thick rope or cable used for towing.

Jib-Boom - Mast-like pole that extends forward from the peak of the bow.

Keel - A beam running the length of the bottom of a vessel.

Lighter - To remove the cargo from a vessel, this name is sometimes attached to the vessel that the removed cargo is placed into.

List - Leaning to one side.

Mizzenmast - The third mast from the bow.

Peggy - Shallow flat bottom boat similar to a rowboat or johnboat.

Port Side - Left side.

Schooner-barge - Sailing vessel modified to be towed.

Screw - Propeller.

Shoal - Shallow area that creates a hazard.

Spar - Mast.

Spar Deck - The main deck through which the cargo is loaded.

Starboard - To the right hand side.

Steam-barge - An early Great Lakes term meaning steamship, normally small, wooden and driven by propeller.

Texas Deck - The deck atop which the pilothouse is mounted.

Yawl - Small lifeboat or rowboat.

BIBLIOGRAPHICAL SOURCES

ARE THEY GHOSTS?
Sources:
Thompson's Great Lakes Pilot, 1869
"The Great Lakes" 2 Beers &Co. 1899
Sandusky Register, 11/8/1859
Cleveland Leader, 11/9/1859
Detroit Free Press, 11/8,9/1859
Buffalo Daily Courier, 11/8/1859

DOG BARKIN'
Sources:
Thanks to Lt. Commander Griff Hamilton, USN Ret.
Sault Saint Marie Evening News, 7/10, 11/1911
Bay City Times, 7/10, 11/1911
"Namesakes 1910-1911," Greenwood
"Great Lakes Ships We Remember," Vol. II, Van der Linden

The Telescope, Nov.-Dec. 1980, "Benny And The Boom," Graham

"Locks and Ships," Soo Locks Boat Tours 1989

Phone conversation with Tom Farnquist, Great Lakes Shipwreck Historical Society, 8/3/1992

HOURIGAN'S QUESTION
Sources:

Daily British Whig, 11/22,26,28/1879, 12/5/1873

Watertown Times, 5/27/1873

Oswego Palladium, 6/2/1873

USLSS Annual Report, 1880

"History of the Great Lakes," J.H. Beers

TRIP 29
Sources:

Author's trip aboard the *J.L. Mauthe*, c/o The Interlake Steamship Company and Bob Dorn.

"Freshwater Whales," Wright

The American Lakes Series, "Lake Erie," Hatcher

Buffalo Evening News, 1/21, 22, 23/1959

Inland Seas, Spring 1992, "The Pittsburgh Supers," Dewar

"The Fleet Histories Series," Vol. 1 Greenwood

"Namesakes II," Greenwood

"Duluth-Superior, World's Largest Inland Port," Van Dusen

Boatnerd.com

Lake Carrier's Association Report, 3/1997

*NOTE Persons wishing to dispute the events regarding the *Cason J. Callaway* may view the author's unedited video tape and audio tape.

BELLES AND THIEVES
Sources:

Saginaw Morning Herald, 9/2,3,5,9/1879

Huron County News, 9/9,18/1879 11/11,20,/1879

"History of the Great Lakes Illustrated" Vol. I and II
Beers

"Wooden Ship-Building," Desmond

Report of the Chief of Engineers, US Army, 1879, 1884

Thompson's Coast Pilot of the Upper Lakes on Both Shores, 1869

Saginaw's Changeable Past: An Illustrated History, Kilar

Christopher Caplinger, Georgia State University, The Tennessee Encyclopedia of History and Culture, "Yellow Fever Epidemics"

Lake Shore Guardian "Sunken History- the Steamship *Bertschy*" Deb Biniecki, August 2007.

E-mail communication with Deb Biniecki, Garry Biniecki 9/26/2007

Aerial Research Survey by Tim Juhl, 9/21/2007

SIGNED PATRICK HOWE

Sources:

Oswego Daily Palladium, 10/29, 30/1919

Bay City Times Tribune, 10/29, 30/1919

The American Lakes Series, "Lake Huron," Landon

The American Lakes Series, "Lake Erie," Hatcher

The American Lakes Series, "Lake Superior," Nute

The American Lakes Series, "Lake Michigan," Quaife

"Namesakes 1910-1919," Greenwood

"Namesakes 1900-1909," Greenwood

"Great Lakes Ships We Remember," Vol. I & II, Van der Linden

Beeson's Marine Directory, 1920

The Telescope, Nov.-Dec. 1980, "The John S. Parsons Ship Chandlery," Palmer

Phone conversations with Terry Prior, Director, Oswego Historical Society, 6/8/1992, 11/29/1992

Phone conversation with Gretchen Rowe, 8/24/1992

Phone conversations with Lowell Nuvine, Hannable, NY Historian, 11/23, 29/1992

Phone conversations with Dick Pfund and Dale Carrier of the Oswego Maritime Foundation, 11/29/1992

Inland Seas, Summer 2007

E-mail communication with Jim Kennand 9/26,27,29/2007

DRAGON SLAYING
Sources:
"The US Life-Saving Service Heroes, Rescues and Architecture of the Early Coast Guard," Shanks & York
"Wreck Ashore," Stonehouse
USLSS Annual Report, 1877, 1879, 1880, 1902

BACK FROM THE DEAD
Sources:
Duluth Evening Herald, 11/4,5,6,8,9,14,15/1895
Port Huron Daily Times, 9/11,14,16,21,28/1895
10/11,28,29,30,31/1895 11/1,5,6,7,8,9/1895
Duluth Commonwealth, 11/4,5,8,9/1895
Duluth News Tribune, 11/9/1895
Bay City Tribune, 11/11/1895

ICE TRAP
Sources:
Soo Evening News, 4/17,21,24,25,26,27,28,30/1917
5/1/1917
Port Huron Daily Times, 5/14/17
"Namesakes II," Greenwood
"Great Lakes Ships We Remember," Vol.s I,II,III Van der Linden
"Freshwater Whales," Wright
"The Great Lakes Car Ferries," Hilton
"A Pictorial History of the Great Lakes," Hatcher
American Shipmaster's Directory, 194

ABOUT THE AUTHOR

Author W. Wes Oleszewski was born and raised in mid-Michigan and spent most of his life with an eye turned toward the Great Lakes. In the past 12 years he has authored 11 books on the subject of Great Lakes maritime history and lighthouses.

Noted for his meticulous research, Oleszewski has a knack for weeding out the greatest of details from the

W. Wes Oleszewski
Great Lakes Maritime Author
and Research Historian

most obscure events and then weaving those facts into the historical narratives which are his stories. His tales of actual events are real enough to thrill any reader while every story is technically correct and highly educational. Oleszewski feels that the only way to teach history in this age of computer and video games is through "narrative." Along the researcher's path, this author has also become acquainted, sometimes first-hand, with the multitude of ghosts and ghost stories that haunt the history of the lakes. The final product of his efforts are captivating books that can be comfortably read and enjoyed by everyone from the eldest grandmother to the grade-school kid and future historian.

Born on the east side of Saginaw, Michigan in 1957, Wes Oleszewski attended public school in that city through grade nine, when his family moved to the town of Freeland, Michigan. In 1976 he graduated from Freeland High School and a year later entered the Embry-Riddle Aeronautical University in Daytona Beach, Florida. Working his way through college by way of his own earned income alone, Oleszewski graduated in 1988 with a commercial pilot's certificate, "multi-engine and instrument airplane" ratings as well as a B.S. Degree in Aeronautical Science. Along with his writing, he has pursued a career as a professional pilot. He holds an A.T.P. certificate and to date has logged more than 5,000 hours of flight time most of which is in airline category and jet aircraft. Samples of his writing can be found on his website at www.light-houses-lakeboats.com.

Other Wes Oleszewski titles by Avery Color Studios, Inc.

- *Great Lakes Shipwrecks and Lighthouses*
  True Stories of Courage and Bravery
- *Great Lakes Ghost Stories*
  Haunted Tales Past & Present
- *True Tales of Ghosts & Gales,*
  Mysterious Great Lakes Shipwrecks
- *Stormy Disasters,*
  Great Lakes Shipwrecks
- *Ghost Ships, Gales & Forgotten Tales*
  True Adventures On The Great Lakes
- *Mysteries and Histories,*
  Shipwrecks of the Great Lakes
- *Great Lakes Lighthouses,*
  American & Canadian
- *Lighthouse Adventures*
  Heroes, Haunts & Havoc On The Great Lakes

Avery Color Studios, Inc. has a full line of Great Lakes oriented books, puzzles, cookbooks, shipwreck and lighthouse maps, lighthouse posters and Fresnel lens model.

For a free full-color catalog, call **1-800-722-9925**

Avery Color Studios, Inc. products are available at gift shops and bookstores throughout the Great Lakes region.